God
Will See
You
Through

Also by Mary L. Kupferle

Your Help Is at Hand
The Light Will Dawn ... Through Prayer
God Never Fails
Trust in the Goodness of God

God Will See You Through

Mary L. Kupferle

Books

Unity Village, MO 64065-0001

Ninteenth printing 2011

To place an order, call the Customer Service Department at 1-800-669-0282, or go online at *www.unitybooks.org.*

Cover design by Karen Rizzo

Library of Congress Cataloging-in-Publication Data
Kupferle, Mary L.
    God will see you through / Mary L. Kupferle.
        p. cm.
     ISBN 0-87159-284-3
     ISBN 978-0-87159-284-2
     1. Christian life—Unity School of Christianity authors.
    2. Consolation. I. Title.
    BV4501.2.K795   1983
    242—dc20   96-40990
                                         CIP

Canada BN 13252 9033 RT

Contents

God Will See You Through

Be assured, dear friend, in this very moment, God will see you through. God will see you through any challenging experience. God will see you through everything in life. God's presence will sustain you. God's love will reinforce you. God's wisdom will guide you. God's peace will comfort you. Let go all anxiety and every fear, for God will see you through.

Regardless of any test facing you, God will see you through wonderfully. God will see you through safely. God will see you through wisely. God will see you through successfully. God's methods are often far beyond and above anything you can consciously know or conceive of. The Scriptures remind you of this in the words: *"Fear not... my steadfast love shall not depart from you, and my covenant of peace shall not be removed... For as the heavens are higher than the earth, so are my ways higher than your ways and my thoughts than your thoughts."* (Isa. 54:4, 10; 55:9)

The answers you seek will come, not by force or human reason, nor by struggle and strain, but by means of the Spirit ever at work within your mind, heart, soul, body, and life. God will see you through, bringing the right answers through the right channels, at the right time and in the right place. God will work through the right persons and circumstances. God will see you through in the best way and for the greatest good of all concerned.

Release all fear, doubt, and anxiety; remember that God will see you through. God will provide all you need of peace, strength, wisdom, patience, faith, and courage. God's love will see you through, not just adequately but wonderfully.

Not long ago when I faced the personal loss of a beloved family member, one who had always been to me a pillar of strength and en-

2

couragement, a solid rock of faith and steadfast love, I wondered how I could rise above
overwhelming feelings of aloneness. In moments of greatest need, and searching for
help, I realized that only God could see me
through. God could and He did. When I needed strength it was provided. When I needed
peace, He supplied it. God brought me
through the experience with greater faith
than ever in His goodness, love, and ever-
present support in every way.

Yes, dear friend, God will see you through,
always, in everything.

Remind yourself now and daily: *I am my
Father's child. He is watching over me, protecting and guiding me. He blesses me with
His presence and power. God is with me to
help, heal, supply, and enrich me. God is
ready and willing to see me through.*

Constantly and consciously remind yourself of this Truth. Take a few minutes each
morning to establish your thoughts in this
positive attitude, confirming and reaffirming
your belief in the goodness of God, the goodness of life, and the innate goodness in all persons. In this way you will be readying yourself to receive God's help and support, to be a
channel through which God can fulfill the

3

highest and best for you.

In another instance of personal need, I again turned to the words *God will see me through* as a rod and staff to hold me secure in faith when no answers seemed forthcoming and every avenue of help was either delayed or closed. It was necessary to continue with these words for days, weeks, yes, even months; but I knew that the Father had the answer and that it would come. God would see me through. One evening, turning again to God's presence within me, I spoke aloud, softly, but firmly: *Dear Father, I know that of myself I cannot do this, but I know that You can. It is not by might or power, but by Your Spirit that the answer will come. You will see me through. Thank You, Father.* At that moment the phone rang and within a few minutes the entire situation was beautifully resolved in ways that dovetailed perfectly to fulfill the needs and desires of others as well as my own. Only an all-knowing wisdom could have worked things out so harmoniously and happily.

No matter what the circumstance, how difficult or how impossible you feel it may be, God will see you through. If life is demanding strength that you think you do not have, wis-

4

dom you think you do not possess, tact, patience, forgiveness, love, or peace that you feel are foreign to you, remember that God will see you through with His strength, His peace, His infinite supply. Tell yourself persistently and firmly that God will see you through, and then let Him.

God will see me through. These were the words, this was the way of prayer, that helped a young woman recently who found herself in a desperate situation in which she was charged unrightfully of business malpractice. She was new in the understanding of Unity principles and asked for help through prayer. As we spoke together, I reassured her that God would see her through safely and successfully. Within a short time and in spite of the fact that her innocence seemed difficult to prove, the case was dismissed. Yes, dear friend, God will see you through.

In another circumstance, the family and friends of a little child, whom physicians had despaired of resuscitating after she had apparently drowned, called for assistance in prayer. All of us who knew of the need immediately stood firm in the declaration that God would see the child through. The next report

5

was that she was in a coma and that even if she lived there would be brain damage. For several days the reports continued in a negative vein: "She is regaining consciousness, but we are not sure of recovery"; "She is trying to speak"; finally, jubilantly, "It is a miracle! There is no brain damage. She will have full and total recovery."

Yes, God will see you through.

Jesus believed in the power of the Father to see Him through every challenge. As He maintained His quiet stand of trust, miracles occurred. As He moved forward in faith, healings came to light and multitudes were fed. His resurrection became a living testimony for all time so that His followers could continue to believe that God would see them through anything.

Yes, dear friend, God will see you through. God will see you through darkness to light, uncertainty to confidence, sickness to health, sorrow to joy, confusion to peace, anger to understanding, fear to faith, lack to plenty, and depression to upliftment. God will see you through all challenges, through any test or trial to victory. God will see you through.

Awaken in the morning with the words upon your lips: *God will see me through.*

Whisper them again at night, and throughout the day hold them in the secret closet of your mind. As you do so, daily, faithfully, persistently, and thankfully, you will know the nearness of your Father and the greatness of your inner Self, made in His image and likeness.

You will be quickened in the realization that it is not of yourself that you accomplish the fulfillment of the good desires of your heart, but by trusting in the power of God and knowing that God will see you through. You will become aware that it is indeed the Father abiding within you who does the work, and you will rejoice to know it.

As you remember that God will see you through, you will be free of burdens. You will see God at work in your personal life, in your family, in your business relationships, and in the simple everyday tasks. Every facet of your life will take on new value and meaning and purpose. You will awaken to a new understanding of what it means to be a channel of God's presence and power.

Let go, dear friend, and trust God. Let go and know that God will see you through.

God Is in Control!

Do you sometimes feel as though everything in your life needs new direction and improvement? Do you long for God's wisdom, order, and healing power to work through your mind and body, for His love and peace to fill your heart? Your life can change if you will quietly know, this very moment, *God is in control!*

You will never, under any circumstance, doubt your ability, feel inferior or defeated, if you will frequently, firmly, and strongly decree: *God is in control!* Then, let go, and *let* Him be!

Stop thinking of yourself as weak, sick, or afraid. Claim God as your Father. See God in control of every cell and atom of your being. Let go, and let God be in control.

This moment, no matter to what extent your human emotions of discouragement, loneliness, or feelings of emptiness want to take charge, stop their activity within your mind and heart quickly with the words: *God is in charge. God is in control.* Claim this Truth strongly and insistently. Demand of your mind that your mind know it! Demand of your feelings that your feelings feel it! Decree and affirm silently and aloud, lovingly and persistently: *God is in control.*

As you consciously choose to know that God is in control, and let Him be in charge, you will rise out of old patterns of limited thinking and negative feelings more quickly than you ever believed possible.

As you turn to God for guidance, divine wisdom will fill you with supreme assurance. When you turn your body, life, and affairs over to God's control, you are then a free channel for the expression of healing, order, joy, and success. You are turning yourself over to the higher thoughts and the higher ways of God, and to the presence and power of God's love that is within you always.

Many times, in the face of some challenge,

I have sat quietly in inner attention to the ever-present Spirit of the Father within, using repeatedly the words: *God is in control,* until the idea has nucleated a strong feeling of substance or life. Newborn strength, faith, and conviction have followed. Sometimes this has come quickly as an inrush of renewal, and sometimes more slowly but just as surely, bringing with it a solid feeling of the reliability and steadfast presence of the Father.

Jesus put the Truth in still another way when He told us that as we lose our life we find it, meaning that as we loosen our hold on limited concepts of life, we find the unlimited reality of our true spiritual selfhood. We will have turned over the control to the Father whose power flows through us as right action and happy results in every detail of daily living.

When the Master sought to help His listeners understand Truth, many resisted because they could not yet comprehend God as being a close and intimate presence and power, woven within the fabric of their minds, hearts, bodies, and lives.

The old concept of an awesome God who rewarded and punished, who occasionally came down from above to bless or to vent wrath, was etched so deeply within their thinking that it seemed unlikely, even with the evidences of miracles of healing, they could let their thinking be altered or face life in a new light of understanding. To acknowledge for themselves that they were one with God seemed blasphemous, for they could not conceive of the power of God as residing within their mortal-appearing, limited-looking selves. To be a good person, or to be kind and understanding, God-fearing and religious, was a possibility, but actually to possess the very power of God within them was beyond their comprehension or desire to accept.

Yet, this was the very purpose for which Jesus came and taught and demonstrated and lived. He knew what all persons can know, practiced what all persons can practice, and expressed what all persons can express when they give God control of their lives.... *for he taught them as one who had authority, and not as their scribes.* (Matt. 7:29)

In one instance, remembering His words, I turned to the inner Presence for the peace, strength, wisdom, love, and poise so deeply needed in the face of a challenging emotional experience. At first, I did not see how help could come, but I kept affirming in faith: *God is in control . . . God is in control . . . God is in control.* Consciously giving up my thought patterns of inadequacy and doubt, and relying upon God to provide what I needed, every smallest detail seemed to fall into place. I had a sense of being divinely directed. The results could not have been more orderly, successful, and beneficial!

When God is in control, the utmost good comes through to bless everyone concerned.

When you practice giving your financial affairs into God's control, when you regularly give your obligations into God's control, when you give your emotional entanglements into God's control, your undesirable habits into God's control, your ordinary routines, home, business, desires, ambitions, and plans into God's control, you are invoking infinite wisdom, divine love, supreme joy, and infinite peace. Then, only the best can result for you.

Jesus tells us that our Father knows our needs even before we ask. The perfect solution to every problem comes from God. Healing comes from God, relief from every burden comes from God. Our part is to consistently, regularly, and faithfully practice giving God full control of our lives.

This does not mean that we become automatons. Rather, it means that we become willing vessels and open channels through which God's power will flow in just the unique and individual way that is right for us.

If we are one with God, this oneness can demonstrate itself only as we let it do so through our receptivity and willingness to let God's power flow through us. This is the way all authority is given to us, through our readiness to be channels for the miracle-producing power of God.

To be such a channel, affirm, the first thing in the morning: *All through this day, God is in control.* And, as you proceed through the day's activities, turn your thoughts to the idea, repeating silently or audibly: *In every detail, God is in control.* Moment by moment, let divine love, wisdom, peace, and joy be the inner controlling power of your actions, your reactions, your words, and your feelings.

If things do not go as you personally had hoped, or if you seem to meet with disappointment, discouragement, and frustration, continue to place yourself and everything and everyone under God's control, persistently repeating: *God is in control. Nothing but the best can result, for God's law of good is always working for the highest good of all.*

In one instance as I sought to do this, I found myself not quite willing to give up my pursuit of a specific goal. But knowing from past experience how much better God knows my needs than I, I finally turned everything over to God, saying, "All right, Father, I thought that this way was best, but now I give everything over to You. You are in control now, all the way." Quickly things turned in an unexpected direction, different from my original plan, but each unfolding detail brought new blessings, and the results were richer and more beneficial in more ways than I could have planned or anticipated.

Form the habit of speaking the words *God is in control.* Inwardly check with divine wisdom before making any move or any decision, asking, "Father, is this the right way? Is this the step to take? Is this what You want me to say?" The answer will come as inner guidance and intuitive leadings.

It is amazing how the details of a day flow smoothly and in order when you give God the opportunity to take charge of your life and affairs. Things are done more easily, accomplished more successfully, and all kinds of added benefits result.

As you give God control of your life, you will feel lighter, less anxious, happier, and less pressured, and you will be assured of the guidance, direction, and good you seek. The repetition of the words *God is in control* will help you let go of tense strivings and fill you with a new awareness that you can truly trust God's guidance in more and more details of your daily life.

Everything Is Working for Good

If you are feeling doubtful, unhappy, or concerned about something, take heart. Hold firmly to the thought: *Everything is working for good.*

If you are frustrated by personal challenges or apprehensive about yourself for some reason, do not be discouraged or dismayed. Know in this very moment: *Everything is working for good.*

This means that specifically and definitely, no matter how difficult, insurmountable, or overwhelming a situation or circumstance seems to be, good is in it. Even if you do not see how this can be, tell yourself: *Everything is working for good.* Regardless of how impossible this statement sounds to you, say it anyway: *Everything is working for good.* Speak the words aloud or speak them silently and in faith. Speak them even when you cannot seem to believe them. Speak them when reason argues with you that there is no way some circumstance or event can possibly bring good into your life.

God is the everywhere, constant, all-inclusive and eternal presence of good, and God is right there where you are, now and forever.

A friend, new in the study of Truth, said to me recently: "I am just now beginning to see that a good purpose has been working throughout what was a heartbreaking challenge in my life. I have met people who have shown me how to think and pray with new faith and effectiveness. The results have been miraculous. Former bitterness has turned to understanding. My entire family has benefited, and the grief-filled experience has opened up to me a new awareness of the value of my own identity as a worthy child of God, able to cope with life and to be happy."

Another friend commented: "Last January when I talked with you several times about the especially difficult trial in my life, I was very upset, as you know. Your reassurance that it was all working for good helped to straighten out my attitude. I started to affirm this every morning for fifteen minutes and I now enjoy life as I never before dreamed possible. You will be happy to know that everything worked out in a natural and beautiful way. Everything has indeed worked for good.''

In both instances, these friends needed to insist within their own thinking that all things were working together for good and they also needed to persist in knowing it.

The importance of persistence in prayer is stressed in Jesus' parable of the widow who kept coming to the judge, insisting that he *"vindicate"* her against her *"adversary."* Jesus opens this parable with the reminder that we *"ought always to pray and not lose heart."* The parable concludes with the words: "... *will not God vindicate his elect...? Will he delay long over them? I tell you, he will vindicate them speedily."* (Luke 18:3, 4, 7, 8)

Yes, God will vindicate us, that is, set us free from bondage to negation. We shall be set free more speedily than we imagine possible when we persist in our prayers, when we insist upon our thoughts turning to Him in faith, when we hold fast to the Truth that everything is working for good.

Charles Fillmore, cofounder of Unity, in speaking of our right to prosperity, puts it in these words: *Banish all thoughts of being a martyr to poverty. ... Think prosperity, talk prosperity, not in general terms but in specific terms ... as your very own right. Deny every appearance of failure. Stand by your guns ... in the very face of question and doubt, then give thanks for plenty in all your affairs, knowing for a certainty that your good is now being fulfilled in Spirit, in mind, and in manifestation.*

At times, when difficulties continue in spite of your earnest prayer, it may seem easy to become discouraged, to become lax in using the rod and staff of the principles of Truth as given by Jesus Christ. Then, more than ever, you need to stand by your convictions, to believe in the ever-present goodness of God in your life. It is all-important then to establish yourself in a deeper awareness of the teachings of the One who knew the goodness of the Father of us all. To do this requires daily insistence and persistence in turning your thoughts to His direction and following through consistently, regardless of what may appear to be happening to the contrary in your life.

Everything is working for good in your life. Believe this. Decree it. Speak it. Insist upon it. Persist in believing it. Be consistent in following through after speaking these words, by listening within for God's direction. Pursue the ideas that come to you with every action you take. Follow the Truth that Jesus taught in thought, word, and action, for He is the one who brought the miracle-working power of God into evidence to remind us that there is always a way through every trial, challenge, and difficulty in life.

You may protest that this is not easy to do. I know, dear friend, but do it anyway. Take heart and know that every bit of persistence and faith will pay big dividends. It did 2,000 years ago and is still doing so today in the lives of those who consistently seek to follow the teachings and principles of Jesus Christ.

The love of your Father never slumbers nor sleeps. His miracle-working power is constantly present, working, moving, producing, and urging you to accept its benefits. Whether you are consciously aware of it or not, it is where you are now. It is blessing you, your life, and activities now. It works as speedily in outer ways as you let it work, by your persistence in consciously knowing that everything is working for good.

Prayer is not for the purpose of changing God but to help us turn our innermost thoughts and feelings into the conditioned state of awareness that enables His healing, strengthening, peace-giving presence to work through us. When Jesus told His disciples that they *"ought always to pray and not lose heart,"* He was saying in effect that we are to persist in believing that everything is working for good.

It is easy to do this when things seem to be going fine in your world. However, when you are feeling low, irritated, hurt, or unhappy, or when you are feeling frightened or insecure, it is an act of faith to stand steadfast and remember that good is at work in all. You can know it again and again until it is a habitual trend of thought and feeling with you. *Everything is working for good.*

In a particularly challenging personal experience in my own life, I tried to maintain this kind of attitude to the best of my ability, yet found discouragement creeping in because the good results were so slow in coming through.

One morning I quietly prayed for light and understanding, for the strength to persist in knowing that everything was working for my good. As I prayed and listened within, it became increasingly clear to me that I had been accumulating all kinds of reasons why things could not work out for my good, why I could not overcome the challenge facing me. I had accepted them as normal reasons to be fearful, as logical reasons to be discouraged, to feel unable to cope, as understandable reasons why I could not be strong enough or peaceful enough to do the things needing to be done.

As light and understanding dawned, I saw in amazement the trend of thinking that had gathered momentum without my being aware of it. I saw that I had somehow chosen to believe all those reasons, chosen to continue to think and feel the opposite of that for which I was praying.

From that time forward it was as though I turned full circle in my thinking processes. I was able really to accept the Truth that everything was working for my good. I could see that even the struggle itself had been producing greater understanding and strength of conviction. This proved to be one of the greatest growing experiences of my life and a period of great blessing and gain in outer ways as well.

Take time to be quiet, to be still and contemplate the Truth that God's love is right there with you, that His light is now shining throughout your mind to reveal what you need to see and know. Listen within and let His wisdom gently turn your thoughts over and over until the questions become answers, the doubts become newborn faith. You will see that everything has been and is working for your good.

Remember Isaiah's promise:

"Every valley shall be lifted up,
    and every mountain and hill be made
        low;
    the uneven ground shall become level,
    and the rough places a plain.
And the glory of the Lord shall be
        revealed,
    and all flesh shall see it together,
    for the mouth of the Lord has
        spoken."

(Isa. 40:4)

All things are working together for your good. This is true right now, the next moment, the next day, and on into eternity.

You are an infinitely beautiful child of God, His offspring, His beloved. Through experiences of life you are growing and you are unfolding the great potentials that are within you.

Everything is working for good. As you insist upon consciously knowing this, as you persist in remembering it daily, you will consistently move forward in faith, and nothing will be impossible. Everything is even now working for your good.

Just as You Are—God Loves You!

Just as you are, God loves you. No matter how unimportant you think you are, regardless of how wrongly you think you have handled anything in your life, how little faith you seem to have, or how inadequate you feel, God loves you.

You are an integral and vital part of God's creation. You were created in His image and likeness, even though you may not as yet be aware of your spiritual heritage.

God loves me. Let these words be written upon your mind. God loves you. You do not have to measure up to anyone else's expectations of you in order for God to love you. You do not have to be something others think you should be or something different from what you now are in order to merit God's love. Just as you are, God loves you.

A young friend told me recently of a challenge in his life through which he became aware, for the first time, of the greatness of God's love for him and of the closeness of God's presence.

He had unexpectedly been faced with the loss of someone he loved more dearly than anyone in the world. There was nothing he could do outwardly to regain this relationship, nothing anyone else could do to put the pieces of his life together again.

For days and weeks he neglected a new, growing business as he prayed and grasped inwardly for peace of mind and for the solutions which did not seem to come. After three months, in total desperation, he decided that life was not worthwhile, that he could not continue the struggle, and secluded himself in preparation for ending it.

Continuing to relate the story, he said in great earnestness: "It was then that the things I had been taught years ago in Unity began coming back to me. Three conclusions came involuntarily to mind.

"First, I began to see that I would be letting down all the people who had ever cared about me. Second, it became clear that I would be going against everything I had believed about the orderly unfolding of my own evolving self. Third, it was also a startling realization to know suddenly that I could not bypass this learning experience, that if I did not face it now, I would have to face it later, somewhere, sometime.

"In those few moments of clarity, after months of emotional upheaval, struggling, and praying, all the stress and turmoil dissolved. I was able to breathe deeply for the first time after almost forty hours of continuous prayer. I literally felt a lifting of every weight from my mind and heart, even a sense of bodily relief. I was free and enfolded in a supreme and overwhelming love that is beyond comprehension or description."

He continued, saying that a new love for life burst through within him, a feeling such as he had never before known. He said that the desire came to him to simply give his best to life and to leave the rest to God and to God's plan for him. He knew that, even though the outer facts might not change, he had changed within, and all things were made new through the love of God experienced in

27

that miraculous moment.

Just as he was, God loved him. All throughout the days he had prayed seemingly without answer, God loved him. While he was trying to come to grips with himself, his situation in life, his mistakes, failings, and inadequacies, God loved him. He knew then that even during the periods of his forgetfulness of his basic faith, his time of skepticism, despite his questionings and agnostic attitudes, God loved him.

This awareness of God's love was evident in the radiance about this young man, in his present approach to his own life of service and his understanding of others. His business has blossomed into undreamed of success since this awakening, and through it he is inspiring and giving to those around him. He knows God as love and that God has a good plan for his life and affairs; and he is following with total acceptance that plan of good.

When you, dear friend, go through a challenge in your life that perhaps hurts you, brings you frustration, makes you weep or despair, struggle or strain, rebel or protest, remember that the same love this young man felt you can feel because God loves you.

If there is something you long for, something you long to see fulfilled, remind yourself: *Just as I am, God loves me.* Remember that you are worthy of good.

You are worthy of the best in life, as God's heir and joint heir with Christ. You are worthy of healing of any physical ill. You are worthy of success in your chosen field. You are worthy of happiness, of enjoyment of every life experience. You are worthy of enjoyment of right companionship, right associates in business; you are worthy of pleasurable moments every day.

Just as you are, God loves you. In this realization you grow stronger, more peaceful, more stable, more understanding, more loving, more giving. You know that nothing stands between you and your good. You are worthy of learning and expressing the things you desire to learn and express.

Tell yourself this day that God loves you, that He is pouring out His good upon you. Accept the ways and means that God will open up to you to bring you fulfillment. Accept His promise as given you through the words of Jesus Christ: "... *I came that they may have life, and have it abundantly.*" (John 10:10)

God loves me. Accept these words. Go all the way in your belief that God loves you, that you are needed and important to Him. Commit your ways and your days to Him who knows you better than you know yourself.

God has fully prepared you for all, yes all, of life's journey. You already have within you all that you need to face everything in life. The more fully you accept this Truth, the freer, happier, and more peaceful you will be.

In your acceptance of God's love, His life, His guidance, all the wisdom, strength, peace, and power you need and desire will flow through you. You will become aware of the miracle of life, of your own true self as you were created—a beloved child of God.

Remembering, *Just as I am, God loves me,* will see you through every experience in life and take you through in dominion, peace, and joy. You will discover the victorious spirit that is within you. You will see yourself as you are in your spiritual self, an overcomer, a beloved offspring of the most High.

You Will Find Your Answer

If you find yourself faced with the need to make a decision, know that you will find your answer. There is nothing in your life experience that can remain clouded, confused, or impossible of solution when you know firmly: *There is an answer, and I will find it.*

At this very moment release every doubt or fear and take hold of the strong conviction: *I will find my answer.* Let go any feeling that you are too involved, too busy, too young, too old, too ignorant, too discouraged, or too weary. Affirm: *I will find my answer.* Continue to decree this silently and aloud. If thoughts of the problem seem overpowering, if feelings of a negative nature want to take over, affirm with authority: *I will find my answer.* Morning, noon, and night, let your attention turn and return to the simple declaration: *I will find my answer.* Then relax, rest, and give thanks to the Father that He will show you the way.

As you continue this practice, unswervingly, persistently, you will find your answer, the desirable solution will be revealed, and many other questions will be answered as well. You will find your answer and be at peace. You will find your answer and realize that you have new inner control. You will find your answer and become aware of gains in patience and faith. You will find your answer and feel new love for yourself and others. You will find your answer plus new perspective and understanding. Your life will open up to new joy, freedom, and contentment.

Release any thought that you should not or cannot see, know, and understand yourself or others, or certain happenings in your life and affairs. As a child of God you can understand what you need to understand, you can know what you should know, and you can find the answers to any questions arising within your mind and heart regarding anyone or anything. You are God's creation of love and wisdom, with intelligence and spiritual comprehension within your very being.

You do not live in a world of ignorance, darkness, and confusion. God's light is within you. When you quietly recognize this, you are returning to . . . *the true Light, which lighteth every man that cometh into the world.* (John 1:9 A.V.) Be assured that this light will bring you the answers you seek.

The answers to your questions will come in a variety of ways, for the Father is not limited. Sometimes your answer will come within the first few moments of your declaration. The light you long for will be there. Perhaps the phone will ring, a letter will arrive, some person will appear, or some event will occur—whatever is right and orderly and for your highest good. The answer will be there and you will see it.

On other occasions, your answer will come gradually, step by step, moment by moment, unfolding in a pattern of developing understanding of yourself, of your relationship to the Father and to life. This manner of answering can often be most lasting and satisfying, so release all sense of haste, impatience, or anxiety in your seeking. The most vital answer of all is the inner answer, the awakened thought, the illumined feeling, the inspired quickening within you concerning the wonder of your own being, the beauty of your own soul's potential, the grandeur of your individual life, progress, and evolvement.

In my own personal experience I have found that some of the most powerful answers to my questions have come over a period of time as I exchanged feelings of haste and pressure for a quiet, continuing, uninterrupted faith and persistence. Seeking for light at one such time, I thought that I had found the answer and began rejoicing. But rejoicing soon turned into disappointment. After further prayer I realized that I had only stepped upon the threshold of the answer. As I let go discouragement and moved on in determination, I recalled and held to the words of Jesus, the master seeker and finder: *"Ask, and it will be given you; seek, and you will find; knock, and it will be opened to you. For every one who asks receives, and he who seeks finds, and to him who knocks it will be opened."* (Matt. 7:7, 8)

Continuing to remember this, continuing to affirm, to give thanks, I did find my answer. The understanding became clearer, the perception steady and progressive. Taking each moment step by step in praise and faith brought me into a richness of blessing that was worth every bit of the effort.

You will find your answer. This is one of the most helpful affirmations you can voice for someone else. If you have tried in every way to help another without results, use this prayer for the person you care about. In a moment of quietness, decree: *You will find your answer.* Then release and let go, and know that the answer will come.

The answer may not come through you but through another person, by another path, another means, another method, at another time than you had thought best. The blessing for this person may appear in a totally different way than you would have considered reasonable or right. It may come in a very simple way which you would have looked upon as impossible, but it will come in the way that the one in need can best receive. He will find his answer and be at peace, and so will you.

Whatever you are seeking for yourself, dear friend, you will find that there are steps to follow, ways to go, and that help is at hand. As you use and work with these steps and ways and help, you will find that you are gaining in spiritual progress, and your diligence will be rewarding, uplifting, even exhilarating. Seeking your answer will invigorate your whole being. As you daily practice becoming quiet, listening within, you will find yourself renewed and increasingly blessed beyond the receiving of the practical answer to your questions.

In one instance, a friend asked for help in holding to his faith regarding a prolonged legal entanglement that had so pressured him emotionally that he could no longer think clearly about it or pray for himself effectively. As we together held to the faith that he could seek and find, ask and receive his answer, he found peacefulness and faith returning. Within the week he reported, "I can hardly believe it! It is like a miracle. It is the most tremendous experience of my life, and I'll never be the same! My lawyer called and said everything has been totally cleared up in an unexpected way. Not one problem remains!"

Recently, a friend called and asked me to be with her in prayer and faith as her son entered surgery. She said that the physicians, deeply concerned for the patient, could not promise good results, for they were unsure of being able to pinpoint the difficulty.

Again, the prayer was for the right answers for all involved: *You will find your answer.* Within a few days the report came through that the recovery was far beyond the greatest hopes of the attending physicians. They told the young mother, "It was as though a chart had been drawn for us throughout the entire time of surgery. We were amazed at the ease of it all." The recuperation time was half that anticipated as necessary.

"Before they call I will answer...." (Isa. 65:24) *"... lift up your eyes, and see how the fields are already white for harvest."* (John 4:35) Be still and know right now that deep within your heart the answer lies ready and waiting for you to find and accept. It is already there; it is already prepared for you; it is already at work within you, ready to come into expression, to bring forth a harvest of healing, harmony, and opulent goodness within your mind, body, and affairs. You will find your answer.

It may take time, patience, listening, and decreeing to move on beyond your fears and doubts, to rise out of any valley of despair. But as you are willing to ask, to seek, to knock, as you reach higher and delve deeper, as you use all the mental, spiritual, and physical energies at your command, your efforts will be repaid richly in goodness multiplied and increased.

You will find your answer. As you put your trust in God you will find the support you need, the light that reveals, the fortitude to keep on. Moment by moment, day by day, night by night, hour by hour, as you pray and ask and seek and knock, you will find your answer. It will be clear, sure, and good. It will be *your* answer!

You Have What It Takes!

If your life seems at times to be too much for you to handle, remember, dear friend, you have what it takes!

You have what it takes to be patient and steadfast.

You have what it takes to see your direction and know the road to travel.

You have what it takes to regain your well-being and strength.

You have what it takes to be staunch in faith and to trust God.

You have what it takes to be successful, happy, and fulfilled.

You have what it takes to feel the peace that passes understanding within your heart.

You have what it takes to live courageously, victoriously.

You have what it takes to face every situation and condition with an overcoming attitude.

No matter what—you have what it takes!

At one time in my life when the demands made upon me seemed overwhelming, when the many decisions needed were difficult to make, it seemed impossible to relax and let go. Thoughts crowded in faster than I could make affirmations, and there seemed to be no letup to the pressure of events. At that particular time, when kept awake at night by doubts and questions, I found that a most healing and helpful thought was: *I have what it takes to relax and let go. I have what it takes to trust God.* Knowing this, I was able to relax and go to sleep quickly.

During the day when the demands seemed relentless, again I found it helpful to remember: *Whatever wisdom I need, I have it. I have what it takes.* This thought sustained me and gave me assurance that saw me through crises, changes, and challenges. I found that I did have what it took, and as a result all things resolved themselves, good came forth, and I was better in every way as a result of the experience.

You, too, dear friend, have what it takes. You have what it takes to face every demand and to know that the Spirit of God in you is more than equal to anything. You have what it takes to face every task and to know that through the Holy Spirit within you can accomplish all things with ease, wisdom, and success. You have what it takes to be still and know that the only presence and power is God the good.

Your mind has what it takes to be divinely illumined. Your soul has what it takes to be poised, peaceful, and serene. Your body has what it takes to be strong, healthy, relaxed, and free.

When you think you do not have the patience to await the answer to your prayer, you have what it takes to know that the answer will come.

When you think you do not have another ounce of strength to see a situation through to the right conclusion, you have what it takes; the added strength is there at hand.

When you feel that you can never again be happy, you have what it takes to refuse to believe this, to know that a new door of life and happiness is opening to you.

41

In one instance, a dear friend faced a number of serious challenges. Anxious family members watched the situation with great concern and asked me to pray with them. I suggested that we affirm: *You have what it takes to see you through.*

As I prayed for this dear person, I held strongly to this realization, repeating many times: *You have what it takes, for God is within you, the source of everything you need.* Within a short while reports came concerning unusual demonstrations of strength, healing, and joy.

When any crisis in your life looms large, remember that you have what it takes. The panic will fade, the threat will dissolve, the enemy will retreat, and the victory will be felt within your soul. Yes, dear friend, you do have what it takes.

As an example of having what it takes, a few years ago I decided to remove a staghorn fern from an old coconut tree in the backyard and put it in a more appropriate setting. Not being an experienced gardener, I did the best I could with the plant, pulling it from the trunk of the palm tree, then temporarily letting it rest in the shade of the patio where it received rain and air. It looked green and healthy, very much alive.

A friend, knowing of my desire for the appropriate container for the fern, offered to take it to a nearby nursery and have it professionally potted. Glad for the assistance, I released the fern into her care. Within a few days she reported difficulty in finding anyone who would pot the plant, saying, "They don't believe it will survive. They say it has no roots." We questioned this verdict and then laughed together in agreement. "Where there seem to be no roots, the roots will grow. God will provide the roots." It took several weeks before she finally found a nurseryman who agreed to try to pot the fern. He did it with reluctance, remarking, "I'll do my best, but it has no roots."

Today, two years later, the staghorn fern is still growing, thriving, a beautiful reminder that where there seem to be no roots, God will provide them. The roots of faith you need and may not seem to have are there. You have what it takes. The roots of your strength, love, peace, wisdom, joy, and courage are there. Even though you do not feel or see or know this by intellectual proof, remember that you have what it takes. Because you are God's child, you have the roots of His being within you and all about you.

Another friend, facing a most difficult situation in his professional career, felt he could not meet the challenge successfully. As he spoke to me about the many facets of the challenge, what it would take in wisdom, patience, and tact to handle it, to bring it to a harmonious conclusion, I kept knowing for him silently: *You have what it takes. Through God in you, you are fearless, you are an overcomer.*

I reminded him that I believed in his abilities, that I believed he had whatever it would take to solve the dilemma successfully. Months of prayer followed while the various details of the situation were worked out. Finally a phone call came, revealing that everything had worked out in a wonderful way for the highest good of all concerned. Tremendous benefits resulted not only for him but for all involved in the situation.

Yes, dear friend, you have what it takes to throw off old limitations.

You have what it takes to relax and let go. You have what it takes to give the burden to God now.

You have what it takes to respond to God's healing power.

You have what it takes to demonstrate prosperity.

You have what it takes to trust in the good and to patiently let the divine plan unfold.

You have what it takes to face change and upheaval with faith and serenity.

You have what it takes, because built into the depths of your soul is the ability to handle victoriously every challenge of your life.

When there seem to be no roots of faith to hold to, to grow from, to rely upon, remember that God will supply the roots. Your part is to believe this; God's part is to provide all that you need. Deliberately turn away from what others may tell you about what you do not have, what you cannot do, or what you should not expect. Remember that you are not at the mercy of the negative in life. Consistently rebuild your awareness of oneness with the Father through steady acceptance of the positive. Begin with the positive thought: *I have what it takes.* Repeat it. Decree it. Speak it aloud. Hold to it silently. God will give the increase.

As Jesus looked up and gave thanks that He would have what was required to feed the multitude, heal the sick, and to bring about miracles, you, too, can look to the same source, the same presence, the same power, the same Father, the same provider of every good in your life. As Jesus knew that He had whatever it would take to pass through Gethsemane and to rise out of the tomb, so you can know that you, too, have what it takes to walk victoriously through every challenge into the light. As a child of God, you have what it takes!

Open Up to God!

Health, strength, peace, well-being in your mind, body, and emotions, better conditions in your home, success in your personal life and affairs, awareness and expression of your potentials and abilities, better relationships with others—all this and infinitely more is yours when you open up to God.

Wonderful and even miraculous things begin happening to you as you open up to God, as you accept the Truth that God's power is present, available, and real. God is ready to refresh, revitalize, and revive you in every phase of being. God is saying to you: *I have chosen thee ... Fear thou not; for I am with thee: be not dismayed; for I am thy God:*

47

I will strengthen thee; I will help thee....
(Isa. 41:9, 10 A.V.)

Perhaps you face some challenge in your life and you are thinking, "I can't make it through on my own power; I don't have the courage and the faith to keep on." If so, take heart and remember that you are far more than you seem to be. You have spiritual powers at your command that rush to your aid when you open up to God—your help, your supply, your support.

God's power within you supports your highest desires, undergirds your being, sustains your life, opens doors, lifts all burdens, dissolves all blocks, clears every path, bursts all bonds—as you open up to it.

Jesus pointed the way to open up to the presence and power of God within. He told the disciples to tarry in the city until they received power from on high. At that point in their life experience the disciples had just gone through earthshaking happenings. They had been subjected to days of ridicule, hours of temptation to disbelieve all they held dear. Unsure and insecure, they had sunk to the depth of despair during the crucifixion of their leader. Then a period of high exhilaration followed in seeing Him again as the resurrected Lord.

To these men, in these circumstances, Jesus spoke the all-important words of instruction and encouragement: . . . *tarry ye in the city of Jerusalem, until ye be endued with power from on high.* (Luke 24:49 A.V.)

These words reminded them that they would need to abide in a habitation of peace (Jerusalem) until they received the spiritual power of God's wisdom, guidance, strength, and faith needed in the days ahead to accomplish what was expected of them. Jesus reminded them that the revitalizing, renewing, restoring, rebuilding essence of everything imperative to fulfilling their mission was available. As they waited quietly, it would come. As they tarried, they would receive power from on high.

Power from on high is the full and creative power of God, the power that moves through the peaceful, open mind and heart as infinite and total supply to fulfill every call of the soul. Power from on high is the inheritance of every man, woman, and child and is contained within the individual, ready to be received consciously by the one who will tarry in faith and quietness, who will open up to God.

If you have become fearful about any condition in your life, you have simply closed yourself to the ever-present Source that frees and heals you. Become quiet within and open up to the presence and power from on high—to the Self of you above and beyond your limited-appearing self. As you tarry, listening within, waiting expectantly, the light you desire will come through.

Do not be discouraged but take time daily to be still, to tarry in a peaceful attitude. Say softly to yourself: *Open up, my soul, open up to God.* Your whole being will respond, and good will flow through you from the inner fount of Spirit.

When you open up to God, you may be guided to take positive action. In one instance, Myrtle Fillmore, cofounder of Unity, in her search for freedom from disease, was motivated to throw herself energetically into housecleaning, despite her feeling of lack of strength and energy, and found a new surge of wholeness and vitality flowing through her. She opened up to God and received power from on high, and healing followed.

In my own personal challenges, I find that God works in many wonderful ways if I will become quiet, listen, and receive. Often I find it necessary to speak to myself with firm insistence: *Open up, open up, open up to God!* This method helps me to gain the full attention of my sometimes resistant human self. As a result, remarkable healing and blessing have come through time and again.

A friend once mentioned the necessity for providing the right kind of environment for healing, a conditioned environment, conditioned through affirmation and prayer. He took an acorn from his pocket, commenting with a smile, "This acorn is capable of being transformed into an oak tree, but it won't happen in my pocket!"

Yes, a conditioned environment is needed for the fulfillment of the purpose of an acorn. It is also necessary for the fulfillment of the divine idea of healing and blessing you seek in your life and affairs right now.

Power from on high, above and beyond every limitation you may face, is available to you. Whatever your longing—peace, healing, joy, love, life, supply—it is available and waiting your conditioned consciousness of prayer, prayer that is conditioned by tarrying, listening, and expecting power from on high.

There is no situation, no condition of mind

or body that can resist the invitation of the spiritually persistent call: *Open up, open up, open up to God!* Amazing results will follow and miracles of healing will come about. At this moment, open up to God. God has already opened up the windows of heaven for you and is pouring out a blessing so great that there is hardly room enough to receive it. Let it flow through you. Open up and receive. Open up and give thanks.

God Is in This Experience

If you are going through a challenge right now, let me assure you that God is in this experience! He is within you as sustaining strength and calming peace. He is within you as the light of wisdom and perfect guidance. He goes before you as gentle protection and tender love. He is the very substance of supply for your need, the very essence of good that will emerge from the difficulty. God is in this experience!

A few years ago a friend found herself in a severely trying circumstance. She faced divorce from someone she had deeply loved, separation from her children, loss of home, alienation from family members, physical illness, and no assurance of financial support. Daily and hourly, even momently, she deliberately turned from every negative aspect to the faith that God was in the entire experience, guiding, directing, helping, healing, and sustaining her.

She commented recently, "Now I can see that God *was* in the experience all the way through, and that every thing that happened was actually transforming me and my life into something so much better and finer that it still seems like a miracle."

Through prayer, through knowing, "God is in this experience," through releasing everything daily into God's way of outworking, this friend has seen every aspect of her life turn to good. She has found a rewarding profession through which she is of service to hundreds of people daily. Her family ties are more solid than ever. Two serious illnesses are completely healed. Her prosperity and well-being abound, and she has newfound depths of peace, faith, love, and satisfaction. Indeed, God was in that experience!

There were three specific steps this friend followed to help her to work consciously with God, to keep her aware that God was with her every day and all the way through every challenge. You can follow these same steps and find yourself lifted out of any difficulty or trial you may face.

First: *Deliberately take the upper hand.* Instead of feeling yourself a victim of circumstance, at the mercy of the happening, take the upper hand and by firm and strong decree declare: *God is here. God is in this experience.* Deeply and persistently, quietly and thankfully know this each day. As you do so, you will begin to feel a lifting, supporting response from within yourself.

Second: *Consistently turn everything to good.* No matter what seems to be occurring, constantly and faithfully keep turning it to good. Determine to turn every present or past liability into a current asset. Turn it all, again and again, to good. Affirm: *Only good can come, for God is in this experience.* You will find confirmation and evidence of this Truth quickly.

Third: *Trust God's plan for you.* Place yourself and all those concerned under His protective Spirit of love. Visualize yourself, everyone, everything, surrounded by light and love. Take time apart from outer activities each day to rest from all conscious reasoning about the situation. Remind yourself patiently: *God's plan is good. I trust it. He is in full control of the experience.* You will feel a wonderful calm within, and you will see new ways of help opening up.

As you take these three simple steps you will be aware that a strong, new faith and conviction are being born within you, deeper peace is filling you, and outer circumstances are responding accordingly.

As you continue to know that God is in every experience, you will see that truly God is there in the seeming difficulty, in everyone involved, be it child or partner or friend or so-called problem person. You will see that God is there in the appearance of illness or pain itself. You will see that God is there in a time of loneliness or discouragement. You will see that God is there despite the appearance of lack or insufficiency. You will see God in every experience, and His presence and power will come directly through the experience to provide whatever is most needed, helpful, desirable, and good.

The story of Jacob's life in the Old Testament is a reminder that no matter what has happened, no matter how many mistakes we have made, no matter how much trouble we face, God is always ready to help. He is always there in that very time and place and happening, ready to guide, lead, lift, and bring good from the experience. No matter how discouraged or lonely we feel and regardless of the depth of our despair or disappointment, as we turn to His presence, we see that He is there.

During the dark night of his soul, Jacob, in fear and desperation, remembered what he had been taught, that God would bless him in any difficult happening in his life. He awakened and said: *"Surely the Lord is in this place; and I did not know it. . . . This is none other than the house of God, and this is the gate of heaven."* (Gen. 28:16, 17)

Yes, dear friend, God was in that place, and He is today in whatever place you are. Healing is in this place. Peace is in this place. Joy is in this place. Love is in this place. Learning and spiritual awakening are in this place. A whole new world of good is in this place and will be revealed as you awaken to the Truth that God is in this experience.

Regardless of who or what seems to be hindering your good, begin now to praise and give thanks that God is in this place. Take the upper hand! Turn it all to good! Trust the goodness of God and His plan for you.

Perhaps you have been thinking, "When I get out of this situation, then I will be at peace. After this is over, then I'll be happy. If I had more faith, then I could handle this situation better. When I understand more, then I'll feel reassured." If this has been your thinking, decide now to change such thoughts to simply knowing that God is in this experience right now. You need not wait another day or hour or minute to know the Truth that God is in this experience. The more certainly, quickly, and fully you accept this, the more certainly, quickly, and fully will God work through the experience to transform and lift and bless you and everyone and everything concerned.

It was this kind of realization that helped me, personally, through a number of challenges some time ago. In one instance of personal hurt and disappointment, I found that the realization of God with me in the experience brought me quickly to the understanding that I could cope with and understand the experience, and learn and grow through it. Since God is in every experience and God is good, only good could come from the experience. This was what I needed to remember, and it brought quick awareness that the challenge itself was the gate of heaven, the open door to greater good. And so it was.

In another instance I found myself in need of physical renewal, and after following the three steps mentioned, new light came through, new revelation brought about all that was needed to effect healing both within and without.

I have seen blessings of peace, light, and understanding, healing of body, healing of finances, healing of relationships come through easily, sometimes almost miraculously. Knowing that God is in the experience is truly a wonder-working awareness.

When Jesus calmed the waves it was through His inner knowing that God was there as peace. When He healed the lame and blind and lifted the multitude to life and health it was because He saw the presence of God there as life. He received strength to overcome challenge after challenge because He knew that God was in the very midst of the happening itself. Knowing this brought Him triumphantly through Gethsemane and the Crucifixion and into our lives today as an ever-resurrecting presence and power. And what He knew then He wants us to know today: *God is in every experience of life.*

Right where you are in your life experience, God is there. He is ready to open up the gates of heaven for you to see the Truth about yourself, which is that you are His beloved, His image and likeness, able to cope, to overcome, to move victoriously through every happening. *"Surely the Lord is in this place. . . . This is none other than the house of God, and this is the gate of heaven.*

Thank You, God! Thank You, God!

Whether your heart is filled with thanksgiving at this moment, or whether it is filled with unhappiness, discouragement, or fear, these words are for you. *Thank You, God! Thank You, God!*

What is your need right now? Is it for healing, supply, guidance, peace? The words *Thank You, God!* spoken and affirmed, silently and aloud, will charge your being with new assurance, peace, and the awareness that good is happening to you at this time and in the present circumstance. As you repeat *Thank You, God!* you will have a new feeling of oneness with the Father and a new confidence that you can meet, face, and overcome victoriously whatever needs to be met, faced, and overcome.

Thankfulness is a builder and strengthener. Thankfulness is a healer, a multiplier of the good, and a dissolver of the negative. Thankfulness is a lifter and a life-giver. Thankfulness is a fortifier and a comforter. Thankfulness is an attracting power for blessings, a lightener of any load or burden, an ingredient of Spirit that produces miracles in the life of anyone in any situation.

Sometime ago when I was experiencing a distressing mental, emotional, and physical challenge, the affirming of *Thank You, God!* brought me through, bridging the gap between doubt and inner knowing, discouragement and upliftment, fear and faith. During this period of months spent in seeking, listening, and following guidance from within as I could best understand it, thankfulness helped more than any other method of prayer. I found it to be a miracle-working process of thought and feeling that brought about inner transformation, then outer healing.

Thank You, God! earnestly voiced again and again built for me a strong ladder of consciousness on which I could climb upward toward the light of Truth to find answers, help, and healing desired. It can do the same for you!

Let these words *Thank You, God!* lift you up right now! Let them bring you out of the darkness into the light. Let them build for you a new realization of the powerful potentials that lie within you, ready to come forth through the very challenge you face at this time. Let the words *Thank You, God!* become a habit. Let them start your days and fill your nights, until you consistently think and feel and know thankfulness through and through your whole being, from tip to toe and inside out.

Thank God in the good times and in the bad. Thank Him when you feel like it and when you do not. Thank Him for your environment and for the people around you. Thank Him for the healing of the body and for the growing of the soul. Thank Him and thank Him and then, thank Him again!

Say the words *Thank You, God!* aloud firmly, or whisper them softly, knowing that they are helping you to climb out of every pit of despair up into the light of Truth and reality.

During the aforementioned period of prayer and praising and thanking God for everything, wonderful results came through me for many around me. A businessman, faced with possible loss of his financial holdings, found new guidance and direction, and with a "better than ever" gain in prosperity. Another person, faced with serious surgery, was quickly released from medical care when no sign of the original difficulty was any longer evident. Another man, severely tested by the strain of inharmony, began finding a new inner light and peace, and conflicts in his life were resolved.

A woman related to me the results that had come as a result of her using this idea of thankfulness to help her husband during a severe illness. The physician had said that there was no hope for recovery. The wife daily built her ladder of praise, daily thanked God for healing. The last visit to the doctor for examination brought forth his exclamation, "It's a miracle! A power above and beyond ours has been at work. There is no sign of any disease."

A friend said recently, "I used to spend my time asking 'Why? Why has this difficult thing come into my life?' Now, even though a challenge may take time and patience for its outworking, I put all the energy of my thought and feeling into the words *Thank*

You, God! Sometimes I need to say them a hundred times a day to keep myself up and on the beam. As a result I have an inner peace and freedom that amaze me, good is happening, and daily demonstrations are evident."

Charles Fillmore writes: *The highest form of prayer is to open our mind and quietly realize that the one omnipresent intelligence knows our thoughts and instantly answers, even before we have audibly expressed our desires. This being true, we should ask and at the same time give thanks that we have already received.*

Begin this process now so that miracles can flow into your life and affairs. Say: *Thank You, God!* when even a little light dawns, or a small degree of understanding comes through. Say it in the face of apparent setback or disappointment. Establish, through thanksgiving, the habit of closeness to your heavenly Father, no matter what the condition or circumstance. Continue to say *Thank You, God!* when things go your way, or if they do not. Follow the advice of the Psalmist: *Praise the Lord!... praise him in his mighty firmament!* (Psalms 150:1) and let thanksgiving become the predominant characteristic of your disposition and your day.

If word comes to you concerning dear ones who are having seemingly insurmountable problems, let your first reaction be: *Thank You, God!* knowing that His presence is there and in charge. If someone very precious to you is going through a heartrending circumstance, let your thoughts be constant in their attention on the words *Thank You, God!* knowing that nothing but good can come to this child of the Father.

Do you remember the healing of Lazarus as related in the New Testament? When Jesus came to call Lazarus forth from the tomb, His words were: *"Father, I thank thee,"* and they were uttered before the healing was evident, before Lazarus walked from the tomb! Jesus said that He spoke these words aloud *"on account of"* those who stood by. We need to speak the words *Thank You, God!* aloud on account of the states of mind and heart that may want to hold us back from acceptance of our highest expression of good, on account of timid attitudes that are afraid to ask too much. The very cells of our bodies need to hear *Thank You, God!* Everything within us and without us responds to *Thank You, God!*

Thank You, God! Thank You, God! Say these words when you feel well and when you do not, when you feel lost and when you feel assured, when you do not know the way to go and when you do, when you laugh and when you cry, when you feel filled with faith, and especially when you do not! Persist, persist, until your heart begins to feel a lift and everything in you begins to ring with joy.

When Joshua went forward to conquer Jericho his instructions were to take seven priests, seven horses, and for seven days encircle the walls of the city, with a crescendo of shouts of praise on the seventh day. As a result of his obedience the walls fell down flat. The victory was theirs. There is always a crack in any so-called stronghold of fear or error. As praise surrounds the situation, the strong, sharp edge of Truth cuts through the crack, and the walls crumble.

Thank You, God! Thank You, God! Listen to your own voice say this. Build your ladder of praise. Old negative states of limited thinking will begin to crumble and fall away. You will experience victory—inside and out.

God Is Healing You Now

God is healing you now! It is occurring at this very moment whether you know it or not. You need not have some mystical experience. You need not feel any unusual physical sensation. You need not even be aware of how it is happening. You need only to relax, to let go, and to be assured that it is being done.

If you are facing a healing challenge of any kind, you can be sure God's healing power will see you through. Indeed, it is happening at this instant. God is healing you now! Whether you are in your home, hospital, office, bus, plane, or car, God's great love is there, healing you now. Whether you have a lot of spiritual understanding or a little, whether you are old or young in physical years, whether you have a great deal of faith or little, you can grasp these few words: *God is healing me now.* They can bring you into a realization that will lead you into total healing, total rebirth, and total change of your life experience for good.

The change may come instantly. If you are going through medical tests or are under the care of a physician, you can silently know: *God is healing me now.* God can and does work through anyone or anything in an infinite variety of ways and means to help, bless, and heal His children. You need not question, reason, or seek out the ways. He will open them up to you, at the right time and appropriate moment, for He is already at work within every detail of your life, bringing about healing in every aspect.

If your heart is downcast about yourself or a loved one, know that God is healing you now, that God is healing your dear one now. Decree and affirm this consistently and faithfully, and you will be placing yourself in a receptive attitude, readying yourself to receive. If you are plagued by doubts and fears, and if negative thoughts fill your mind, use the words *God is healing me now"* as a rudder to keep your mind turned in the direction of His presence and power. Remember, the Truth is that God is healing you now.

If you need to speak these words for hours, days, weeks, or perhaps longer in order to let go of limited and negative habits of thinking, the results will be worth every effort. All the way will be a healing way. You may have to stretch your muscles of faith more than you thought you could, but as you do so, knowing that God is healing you now, you will be placing yourself in the position of receiving the greatest blessing of your life.

If you become discouraged, thinking that healing will never come, if you see little sign of progress, quietly realize that God's continuous healing power is at work beyond your ability to judge. Do not reason or compare or try to figure it all out. Instead, deliberately trust that in every moment and in every detail, God is there, guiding, helping, seeing you through to total healing.

To continue to repeat the words *God is healing me now* is to fill the mind and body temple so full of this awareness that there is no room left for fear or doubt. Further persistence in repeating them is to become so fully saturated with this Truth that it begins to overflow your mind and body and fill the atmosphere around you. The very air you breathe, your environment, will begin to vibrate with the power of the thought: *God is healing me now.* Healing will fill the air. Healing will be released within every cell of your body, into every condition in your life, and into the lives of those around you.

Knowing that it is the Father who dwells within you who does the work, you can leave the outworking to Him, regardless of whether the healing is for mind, body, relationships, or any of your affairs. God knows the ways and means to bring the right results. Because things are in the process of being healed, you will gladly cooperate and accept His guidance. Your prayers will have a new spirit of release within them as you inwardly become more aware that in every moment, in every circumstance, in every situation, in every development, in every outworking, God is healing, healing, healing!

I have seen the healing of all kinds of conditions. For every healing in my own life or in the lives of others, I have seen just as many ways these healings have come. The ways of answered prayer for healing are as infinite as God is infinite.

Healings have occurred in every kind of environment, through silent prayer or audible, through strong decrees and gentle, sometimes in church services and sometimes in hospitals, regardless of the religious affiliation or lack of it or the manner of prayer. The ways of God and His healing power transcend our concepts. There is no limit to the healing power of God or to the reach of the healing touch and presence of Jesus Christ.

No matter what any person may say of the impossibilities of healing, all things are possible with God. To acknowledge with praise and thanksgiving: *God is healing me now,* is to let the healing begin to flow. Now is the time to believe it for yourself. God is healing you now!

The Power of a Minute

Minute prayers are possible for anyone to practice. No matter where you are, you can call upon the presence of God. Take that minute, in spite of anything, in the midst of anything, regardless of the place or circumstance.

Take a minute before getting out of bed in the morning. During morning activities, every so often stop for another minute. Quiet your thoughts, anxieties, rushed feelings, and again feel yourself enfolded in the presence of God. Everything that seemed so pressing will become secondary. An awareness of being in control will fill you and you will go forward with order and confidence.

During the noon and afternoon hours, keep faithful with the minute prayer. Stop frequently, and whenever possible close your eyes, looking within to the presence of the Lord, to His light, to His quiet reassurance.

The more rushed you are, the more urgent things appear, the more important it is to stop for one quiet minute in which you turn to the inner light, the presence of God within you.

One minute out of every hour of your working day totals only eight or ten minutes. That seems like a brief time to give to the presence of God! But what a difference it makes in your inner feelings, in your facial expression, in the effectiveness of working, serving, and living.

The minute prayer keeps you on the beam. It brings you out of the rush of the world into the kingdom of heaven briefly, but long enough to taste, touch, and feel the presence of God in a new degree. It disciplines the mind, feeds the soul, heals the body, and prospers the affairs.

Practicing the presence of God through minute prayers enlarges the capacity for receiving the Presence in every detail of life. You find Him in your work, home, body temple, family, and world. You awaken to the Presence everywhere.

As you begin the minute prayer, visualize the light of God enfolding you. See yourself sitting quietly in the light. See yourself rested, receptive. For just one minute, rest there in the light.

You will be amazed at the power one minute spent like this has to bring you into right perspective, to give you new, rich ideas you need, to clear away the cobwebs, to relax the muscles, to bring healing to the body. Everything you find to do afterward will carry with it greater drive, energy, power, love, peace, and success.

If you are lonely, rest in the light, and you will feel the presence of the Lord as love and companionship. You will be directed into the right relationships and at the right time.

If you are angry and upset, rest in the light. You will be astonished at the change in yourself. You will become more gentle and forgiving, and harmony will be effected.

If you are confused and unsure of yourself, rest in the light and you will find a blessed new awareness of confidence and assurance after the minute prayer.

Take a minute! Give a minute! Experience

a minute prayer. Practice the Presence minute by minute. Learn about prayer by the minute. Let your life fall under the control of the minute prayer. It will change everything for the better in miraculous ways.

Listen to the Lord of your being for one minute each hour of the day. As you continue the minute prayers for a week, a month, or longer, the light will make itself known to you. The inner gates of perception will open automatically to the kingdom of God within you. Experience the minute prayer! Experience the power of it, the peace of it.

Take a minute—now!

You Can Understand

Does someone seem to treat you unfairly or unkindly? Have the events of your life taken certain turns that challenge you? When things happen during the day that would be enough to upset anyone, the inspiration of the Almighty, given opportunity, will come forth out of quietness to guide and direct your actions and reactions.

... there is a spirit in man: and the inspiration of the Almighty giveth them understanding. (Job 32:8 A.V.) Through this Spirit within, you can meet any difficulty and have the wisdom to overcome it. You can rise up in new spiritual stature and authority. No matter how young or inexperienced you are, no

matter how long-standing your confusion or perplexity, you can understand, you can overcome, you can rejoice.

You can find the answer to any troubling condition or situation by stopping for a moment of quietness and saying within, "What is this about, Lord of my being?" Just as quietly, inwardly, the Spirit that is in you will reveal what you need to know, will give you words to speak or help you to be still and hold your peace.

There is nowhere you can go without the Spirit of the Lord going with you and before you to make clear your way. There is no one you can meet and nothing that can happen without the inspiration of the Almighty flowing through you to bless you and to bring forth good.

Jesus understood people so well. He beheld the full picture of every situation so truly that He could ask the right question or give the right answer at any time. His kind of understanding can be ours when our prayer becomes His way of prayer, when we are willing to be still long enough to release every question, to accept in its place spiritual understanding, the understanding that we are one with God, that we live and move and have our being in Him.

You will find that your spiritual understanding grows daily as you acknowledge the indwelling Spirit of God, as you know that His Spirit in you gives you wisdom and direction.

You are not meant to control the life of another, nor his movements and reactions, but you can control your own thoughts, feelings, actions, and reactions. In the awareness of the presence of Christ within you and within all persons, you can release your concern about others and replace it with an inner assurance of love and understanding. When you find yourself questioning, say to yourself, "I understand. There is that in me which knows; there is that in me which trusts; there is that in me which beholds the goodness of God at the heart of all, at work in all."

The more you understand yourself and the power of God within you, the more peace, wisdom, love, and joy you are able to express constructively, positively toward others. You can be a dynamic force for good, a channel through which God's power can find expression.

Spiritual understanding is a body healer, a mind and emotion healer. Understanding that flows from the indwelling Spirit of God within you is powerful enough to break every bond, to free every thought of limitation, and to heal any negation.

Spiritual understanding can settle any argument in quietness and harmony; it can meet any hardness of thought and melt it into peace; it can fuse any group of disunited people into amazing oneness of purpose.

Right now you have a spirit in you that has the capacity for spiritual understanding. You can understand yourself; you can understand others—even that in them which has seemed beyond your understanding. You can understand a child, a teen-ager, a parent, a condition.

Say to yourself often, and quietly, "I understand," and then remain receptive and silent, letting the inspiration of the Almighty fill you. You will then be able to speak the words that need to be spoken, to perform the deeds that need to be performed. You will understand; you will be understanding.

What Prayer Can Do for You

Prayer is for anyone and everyone. It is a natural inclination of the child or of the adult. It is not a strange, fanatical, or emotional approach to a problem, but a quiet, Christlike attitude that looks for the good in everything and everyone. It is an attitude of heart and mind that knows there is a good outworking for every challenge.

Prayer is not a mystical activity reserved only for those who feel inclined to express themselves religiously. It is a simple, normal activity of the mind and heart of everyone who desires to be a better person, to understand life and living, and to live more richly.

If you will accept this statement that

prayer is the answer, that prayer is power, and that prayer can change all things that need changing in your life, yourself, or in any condition of any kind, you have placed yourself in the stream of blessing that is available to all who ask in faith, believing.

If you are unhappy, prayer can lift you into a new lightness of heart, joy, and happiness. If you are plagued with resentment and bitterness regarding a person or situation, prayer can bring a new understanding to you that will fill you with new peace and amazing love. If you are fearful, prayer can transform you into a person of great courage. If you appear sick or financially lacking, prayer can heal your body and restore your affairs. There is nothing prayer cannot do for you.

Prayer is an inner line of communication between you and your Creator. Prayer is your inner contact with wisdom, understanding, and inspiration. Prayer is your inner awareness that the Spirit of truth, of which Jesus spoke, is not only with you but within you, ready to teach you all things. "*... the Spirit of truth ... will guide you into all the truth; ... and he will declare to you the things that are to come.*" (John 16:13)

A few moments of being still, quieting your

mind and listening within, will so calm your thoughts that you can pick up your work and activities with renewed wisdom and confidence. A few moments of complete silence, acknowledging the presence of God surrounding you, within you, will bring forth new strength and assurance and will fill your body with fresh vigor and vitality. A few moments alone in stillness, remembering that you are a beloved child of a loving Father, will refresh your whole being and bless your life.

True prayer is an inner attitude, not a certain outer position or posture. Prayer makes no demands concerning time or location. Right where you are, at your place of business, on the street, in the home, you can pray and pray effectively. The presence of God is everywhere at all times. The Spirit of truth is eternally with you and in you as Jesus Christ promised. If you think you do not know how to begin praying, listen within and this Spirit of truth will teach you. If you feel inadequate about praying, be still and obedient and the Spirit within will guide you.

You may say one word, "Father," and you have prayed and will receive your clear answer. You may pour out a heart full of desire and you have prayed and will find your help nigh. You may repeat a beautifully worded psalm and you have prayed and will see your direction. You may say nothing at all, only be still, and you have prayed and will receive.

Moses prayed in his own way, and he received sufficient guidance to lead the enslaved Israelites into the Promised Land. Joseph prayed in his way, and he received wisdom and patience and understanding that brought great success and happiness to him and to all those about him. Paul prayed in his way, and he received great illumination that changed his life and moved the world. Jesus prayed in His way and miracles of healing and blessing became a daily occurrence.

Pray in your way. You will see that your life will be transformed and blessed. Stand on no formality. Do not be ashamed to pray. Do not feel guilty because you have prayed infrequently before. Begin to pray now in your own way, in your own time, in your own place of life, and see what prayer can do for you.

People who pray are illumined people. People who pray are inspired people. People who pray are strong, courageous people. People who pray are happy people. People who pray are successful, confident people. That is what prayer can do for you, for me, for everyone. It will illumine you, heal you, prosper you, and bring you into such peace and joy as you have never known. Pray now and see what prayer can do for you!

There Is Enough and to Spare!

It was when the hungry, despairing prodigal son remembered that in his father's house there was enough and to spare that he said: *"I will arise and go to my father...."* (Luke 15:18)

Do you feel that you lack some good thing? Do you feel that you lack ideas and initiative, patience and understanding, wisdom and direction, peace and quiet, strength and power, substance and fulfillment? If you feel a lack, remember that in Truth there is enough and to spare in your Father's house. There is not just enough, but enough and to spare!

The moment you remember this, you can return to your Father's house, and He will receive you with love and with blessing.

It is through prayer that you arise and return to your Father, God. Through looking to God as the source of all good you find that there is enough and to spare. Take with you into every moment of your day this thought: *There is enough and to spare.* Think of this as you walk, as you drive, as you play.

If a demand is made on you for fresh ideas, declare in faith: *There is enough and to spare.* As you believe that there is enough and to spare, you will be stimulated and inspired with the ideas that you need and can use.

If a member of your family or a co-worker is irritable or difficult, and you need patience and understanding, declare in faith: *There is enough and to spare.* As you believe this, you will find that order is restored and harmony enters into each relationship.

If problems must be solved, if you seek the answer to a question, expect to have enough and to spare of wisdom and direction. If you receive disquieting news, if there are disturbing events, affirm that you and your world are blessed with enough and to spare of peace and quiet.

If you feel a lack of energy and vitality for the day's work, remember you have enough and to spare of strength and power. The very cells of your body will respond to your acceptance of this idea. You will have a surplus of energy with which to enter into and enjoy your activities.

If you appear to be short of money, limited in your supply, remember there is enough and to spare. Your faith that there is enough and to spare, your returning to your Father in prayer, opens the way for an overflowing measure of good to be poured into and through your affairs. You will act as a channel of blessing. Not only will you be prospered but your quickened awareness of plenty will bring prosperity to those whose lives touch your life.

All that the Father has is yours. Say to yourself: "I will arise and go to my Father." Then go. Go in love, go in faith, go with a feeling of thanksgiving. As you go to God in prayer, as you feel your oneness with Him, rejoice in the satisfying knowledge that there is enough and to spare.

You Are Unburdened!

In a moment of quiet, in a time of meditation, in a period of prayer, read and contemplate these words: *I am unburdened. God's love sets me free.*

All cares, doubts, and anxieties are released from your conscious and subconscious minds. You are unburdened through the wonderful power of God's love. His Spirit, active in you right now, sets you free. You are unburdened; you are free!

Whatever has weighed on your mind is now released. All burdens, problems, and responsibilities that have filled your thoughts are now loosed and lightened. You know that you are unburdened; you know that you are free.

Your thoughts soar; you catch a new vision. You understand that the Mind of God, expressing through you, enables you to handle all things wisely, intelligently, and perfectly. You are unburdened; you are free.

If your shoulders have felt laden with cares and obligations, let your prayer be: *I am unburdened. God's love sets me free.* As you pray, your shoulders will relax, straighten, and be strengthened. You will know that you are spiritually capable, spiritually powerful. You will no longer feel limited or cast down. God's love lifts all worldly weight, makes easy all physical demands. Your shoulders are unburdened; you are free.

The cells, nerves, muscles, and atoms of your being are energized into easy, harmonious action and reaction as you continue to remember: *I am unburdened. God's love sets me free.* This thought releases all tension, stress, and strain, and lets each organ function normally and perfectly. This thought frees all tightness, loosens every knot of pain. It harmonizes all bodily activities, and gives you new freedom, strength, and well-being. Your body is unburdened; you are free.

Your heart is released from heaviness. All doubts, all sorrows are cast off. You are filled with the peace that passes understanding. Your heart is unburdened; your heart is set free. In this newfound freedom your heart works in divine order, and its action is perfectly regulated. A wellspring of joy bubbles up within you; you are filled with new faith. Your heart is unburdened; you are free.

You move through every activity, face every challenge, and meet every responsibility with ease and with a peaceful mind. You give every burden to God. You understand and you accept the promise: *"Come to me, all who labor and are heavy laden, and I will give you rest."* (Matt. 11:28)

You now rest—even in the midst of vital activity you rest. In the peace-giving presence of God, you relax, you rejoice. You are completely unburdened. You are now and forever unburdened; God's love has set you free. Accepting His promise you find perfect rest.

God's Law of Adjustment

Are you in the midst of a change in your work, home life, or environment? Are you facing a period of adjustment? Regardless of the nature of the challenge, be it mental, emotional, or physical, God's law of perfect adjustment will carry you through easily and harmoniously.

Remind yourself often: *God's law of perfect adjustment is now making every change smooth, easy, and harmonious. There is no conflict, no resistance. My whole being is in agreement with God. His goodness makes all adjustment of mind, body, and affairs orderly and perfect.*

Know that you are now moving through

each change in the absolute assurance that every adjustment is God-directed, God-eased, and God-fulfilled. Accept this Truth quietly and faithfully many times during the day. Repeat this statement to yourself silently and aloud, saying: *God's law of perfect adjustment now makes every change smooth, easy, harmonious, and perfect.*

No change, adjustment, action, or reaction is intended to be harsh, strained, or difficult. There is no necessity for trying mental, emotional, or physical reactions in response to outer moves and changes. God's law of adjustment stands ready to bless, regulate, balance, and maintain every phase of your being.

We are told by scientists that even a ball thrown into the air requires an adjustment throughout space and creation, so delicate and yet intelligent is the law of natural universal adjustment and balance.

Above and beyond this amazing law of natural adjustment is the great law of perfect spiritual adjustment. This law is momently in action for your individual blessing, constantly in attendance in your life to make your every move orderly, harmonious, and perfect.

Call on this law now by repeating quietly to yourself, *God's law of perfect adjustment now makes every change smooth, easy, harmonious, and perfect.* As you cooperate with this law you permit its blessing to move through your mind, to adjust and heal every emotion. As you cooperate with this law you permit its blessing to move through your body to regulate and direct every body cell. As you cooperate with this law you permit its blessing to move through your affairs and to bring about an easy and natural development in every new phase of living, every new direction your life takes.

The law of life embraces change. Your spiritual, mental, and physical well-being depend on orderly and progressive change. As you accept this Truth in an attitude of nonresistance and in faith, each step will be filled with harmony and success, and you will be uplifted.

Determine this day to move along in the awareness that you are in tune with your good through God's perfect law of adjustment. Know that God's wisdom guides you; God's love protects you; God's life renews you; God's substance supports you.

Remember that God's law of adjustment

works for all of His children as well as it works for you.

Trust God and let His law of perfect adjustment make every change smooth, easy, harmonious, and perfect. Let this law make all things right.

Release It!

Have you been praying about a loved one or a friend and felt your prayers were not adequate? Are you concerned about a condition or a situation in your home, your business, or your affairs? Are you clinging to the thought of how things can be made right, what shape and what form the solution should take? Then release! Loose! Let go and let God!

The prayer of release is one of the most effective prayers we can pray. The prayer of release helps to free us from tightness, tension, and grasping. The prayer of release helps to remind us that God is the doer, not we. The prayer of release helps us to become open, receptive, and obedient channels through which God can work.

Do not hold to you the person you would help. Do not bind him with those things you desire for him. Simply, quietly, and easily release him and his welfare to the loving Father. Pray: *I release you. I loose you. I let go and let God have His perfect way in you.*

Your releasing of other persons does not mean that you care less about them but rather that you care more about them. You are by this very act of releasing placing them in the keeping of the One who is all-wisdom, all-love, all-power, and all-good.

Jesus often prayed such a prayer of release. In the garden of Gethsemane He prayed to release, to loose, to let go, and to let God. He came at that point to an utter and complete release of His loved ones and friends, the situation and circumstances, His own personal desires, and the ultimate outer results. His was a prayer of perfect and complete release, which resulted in the glory of the Resurrection.

Throughout life all of us experience our Gethsemanes, times of doubt, fear, and trial. Through a prayer of release we also experience resurrection in renewed faith, courage, and order. We achieve this resurrection when we come into an understanding and a feeling for the words: *I release, loose, and let go and let God.* Such a prayer accomplishes much for us. It frees us from doubt and helps us to be resurrected through faith. It frees us from personal bonds into an expanded awareness of life. Such a prayer frees us from ties and limitations, and we accept the goodness of God.

Whatever your desire, goal, longing at this moment, turn to a prayer of release: *Release, loose, and let go and let God.* Your longing can be fulfilled, for God has implanted its good concept within your heart. When you cease to place personal restrictions on your desires, when you loose your doubts and anxieties and release them to the Father, then His perfect work can be accomplished through you and for you.

Relax mentally, physically, and emotionally. Say to yourself: *I release, loose, and let go and let God.* Do not be fearful of letting go. Nothing can be lost through spiritual release. Instead, your own good is much freer to move into your life.

Through release your power of attraction for good is increased. Through release your horizons of acceptance of life, love, and wealth are broadened. Through release your mind and heart are opened to receive that which God gives, and your body and affairs become channels for the outpouring of His blessings.

Release, loose, and let go and let God. Take a few moments now, wherever you are, to do this. Give your mind, your heart, your body, your business, your home, your loved ones, and every situation in your life to God. Remember that the Father does the work. The Father is the source of light through which right answers come to each of us. The Father is the giver and the sustainer.

This Is Your Day

This is your day, the day God has prepared for you to live, to love, and to enjoy. Say to yourself as you arise, as you dress, as you eat your morning meal: *This is my day!*

If you have been confronted with difficulties and dread to meet another day, do not be anxious or fearful concerning developments and outcomes, but greet the day with the thought: *This is the day of my overcoming and victory. I will be strong and courageous!* The loving Father will be with you through every moment. His wisdom will abide within you through every hour.

If your heart keeps turning and returning to the past, longing for the good of the past, bring your heart up to date with the affirmation: *This is my day. This is my day of great expectation, my day of joy and blessing!* Through these words you cultivate an expectation of great good now, and you will find that the blessings of the past have been only a foretaste of the infinite good God sets before you today.

If you feel that you cannot see your way, if your problems seem more than you can bear, then declare: *This is the day I give all my burdens and responsibilities over to God. Today I find perfect peace and freedom.* Relax, let go, let God. Let God work in and through you.

If your body seems to need greater strength and health affirm: *Today I accept the fullness of God-life. This is the day of my wholeness and strength. This is my day of renewal.* Realize that this day is a new beginning, a day to rise and walk in a new consciousness of life.

This is your day. You need not be concerned about tomorrow, next month, or next year. Every moment is a new moment. As the moments come, accept them as opportunities to take hold of new faith and courage, new wisdom and love, new joy and happiness.

The more fully you accept God's gift of today, the more fully you prepare yourself for a wonderful tomorrow. The courage you take hold of this moment will build within you a tower of strength for every overcoming. The faith you lay hold of right now will widen your horizons.

This is your day! This is your day to praise and to bless, to give and to receive, to love and to be loved, to laugh, to sing, and to rejoice. Live it fully, live it lovingly, live it freely and joyously, for this is your day!

Sing a New Song

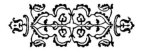

No matter what has occurred before, this is a new day, a new hour, and a new moment. You can take hold of joy on the wings of prayer and find yourself lifted into lightness, peace, and courage.

You are a child of the living God, meant to express happiness, meant to radiate beauty and serenity as bright and lovely as the rays of the morning sun, meant to embody the music and harmony of the universe. Joy is your gift from God, and it is not dependent on what occurred ten years ago, a month ago, yesterday, or last night.

Joy belongs to you, whether you know it or not. It is yours now, to discover, to use, to exercise, and to bring into expression.

I will sing a new song today. As you repeat these words quietly, as you speak them aloud, you will find fresh courage rising within you and newness of hope stirring within you.

I will sing a new song. Tell yourself: *I will let the song burst forth from the innermost part of me. I will let it come forth in a smile. I will let it come forth in tolerance and forgiveness. I will let it come forth in praise for others. I will sing a new song until my whole being thrills with the joy of life and living.*

You can sing your way through this day, and you will find yourself strengthened, not only mentally but physically. This does not mean that you must actually give voice to song—although this is helpful in itself. It does mean that wherever you are, whatever you are doing, you can sing a song in your thoughts, in your heart, and in your soul.

You can do this, your expression will change; your face will shine; it will radiate beauty and youth; your body will move freely and gracefully; your work will go more smoothly; your life and affairs will be blessed and transformed.

All the natural universe is based on principles of harmony, order, and rhythm. An eminent scientist has declared that there is actually music in the spheres, that there is music within every single atom. God is harmony; God is rhythm; God is order; God is joy. The Earth, the other planets, the sun, and the stars move in harmonious, joyful rhythm. When we are filled with joy we are at one with the universe, and the harmony and rhythm of God fill us and inspire us.

Sometimes we think we cannot get into the swing of things, that we are out of step with success, wholeness, happiness, or peace. At such times, it is more important than ever that we realize that the gift of joy is innate within us and can be aroused. Paul says: *. . . stir up the gift of God, which is in thee . . . .* (II Tim. 1:6 A.V.) Stir it up with the words: *I will sing a new song!* You can and you will find a wellspring of joy within you that you never dreamed existed.

You need not wait until some future time to become aware of this inner joy. You need not wait for it to come to you through some person, particular thing, or attainment.

Do not postpone your joy for another moment. Sing a new song of joy today, this hour, this minute. Sing for the joy of the Christ teachings. Sing for the joy of knowing that you are a child of the living God. Sing for the joy of knowing that your loved ones also are children of the living God. Sing for the joy of knowing that you are a spiritual being, immortal, indestructible, changeless, and perfect.

A song of joy is your divine birthright, and a life abundant is your heritage. Declare triumphantly: *I will sing a new song of joy this day. I will sing to the glory of God. I will sing to the upliftment of all mankind.*

Sing a new song this day, a song of joy, and your thoughts will sparkle; your presence will be radiant; your life will be like the shining sun.

He Who Calls Thee Keeps Thee

The heavenly Father who created you and brought you forth is the same Father who will forever sustain you and help you to go forward to your highest good.

Whatever your fear, your discouragement, your problem or difficulty, the Father is with you now, ready to help you arise to victory. You need only turn to Him, open your heart to His loving-kindness, and in that moment you will find new strength and encouragement to go forward, new wisdom and understanding with which to accomplish your task.

Turning to the Father in prayer for help is not a strange or complicated process, but so simple that the Master has told us we need only become as willing and trusting as a little child and we shall find Him. We need not formulate great and beautiful phrases, study long hours to find impressive words, but merely accept a simple utterance such as: *He who calls me keeps me and is the power of my attainment.*

If you are in any kind of need, accept this statement and carry it with you this day. If you have some task to perform that seems especially difficult or important, if you are entering a new phase of life, if you are desirous of receiving renewed health or supply, know that the Father is not only working with you toward success and accomplishment, but He is working within you as well, giving you the inner wisdom and light that makes plain and clear your path.

Whenever you are called upon to do something that seems impossible, say to yourself: *God in me can!* Yes, God can! Regardless of human limitation, personal hindrances, despair, and consternation, God can work with you and within you to solve your problems joyously and victoriously.

Even as the Father worked within Jesus to heal the sick, raise the dead, and bless the multitudes; as the Father worked within

Peter, within Paul, and within all the disciples, as they continued to spread the Master's teachings, so the Father works within you and me today to prove the Truth of all that is good.

God is working with you and within you this moment, so let go of all fear and trembling, let go of all anxiety and dismay, and speak these words of assurance to yourself silently and aloud. Speak them calmly, then know that the Father is by your side, leading, guiding, and blessing you in every step you take, in every move you make. Know that His everlasting arms are sustaining you always, that He is showing you the path in which to walk.

If you long for outer proof of this Truth, if you wish that you might see with your own eyes the "cloud by day" and the "pillar of fire by night" such as led the Israelites out of Egyptian bondage, know that you will be given all the assurance you need in the way you can best accept and use it. Perhaps it will come into evidence as a suggestion from a companion, or it may manifest itself in the form of increased faith or a new idea. The Father has many avenues and channels through which to work, and when we turn to

Him in trust, in prayer, they become apparent and substantial in our lives. Sometimes, however, the greatest proof is in a new surge of courage motivating our thinking, a new power stirring our faith, a new inspiration lifting our hearts.

Take this Truth into your heart, let it replace all thoughts of anxiety, any former prayers of supplication or petition. Hold fast to this Truth in the face of negation. A change will come! The Father will not fail you nor forsake you.

God Is Taking Care of It

Yes, dear friend, God is taking care of it. Whatever your need at this very moment, God in His infinite love and wisdom is fulfilling it and taking care of it.

If you need direction, if you need to know the way to go, direction and guidance are yours. God is taking care of it.

If you are discouraged about the slowness of healing—mind, body, or emotions—lift up your vision to the Truth that right now, without delay, God is taking care of it.

If you need comfort and reassurance, encouragement and support, greater confidence, conviction, faith, light, or understanding in regard to anything in your life, God is taking care of it.

God will take care of you in every circumstance of your life as you quietly let go and let Him. God is caring for you, watching over you, and protecting you. God is renewing and rebuilding you, filling you with His joy, enfolding you with His love.

God is taking care of your smallest need and your greatest desire. God is helping you to release your tensions. God is dissolving your fears. New peace and assurance come to you as you simply, trustingly affirm: *God is taking care of it.*

Your reasoning mind may question, "How can I have the courage to see this through?" "What will ever get through to my dear one's thinking and help him to see the light?" Stop. Stop the questioning. Stop the doubting and wondering. Instead, affirm quickly, gently but firmly: *God is taking care of it.* Affirm it with a sense of finality and completion, knowing that the affirmation is already taking effect.

Let God's love and wisdom take over. You will feel an immediate sense of relief. You will be able to take a deep breath and relax. You will suddenly realize that you do have faith, that you can be at peace, that you are a child of God, heir to all that He is.

Each time you repeat the words: *God is taking care of it,* you will realize that human force and pressure are no longer needed. You will gain a new awareness of what it means to let go and let God. You will see that you have opened up a new area of understanding regarding your true relationship with your heavenly Father. It will become clear to you that you are the channel and that God is the doer of His good works through you. You will feel the effectiveness of your prayers, knowing that God does the work, not you.

Jesus knew this Truth so totally that He was not burdened by the multitude of people or the multitude of problems facing Him daily. He knew that God was taking care of it all. He tells us this in Scripture: "... *the Father who dwells in me does his works.*" (John 14:10)

A wonderful release is felt as you think of these words: *God is taking care of it.* God knows the need and is filling it now. You quickly relax as you realize that God's presence is within you and within the circumstance, resolving it in perfect time and in perfect order. God is taking care of any condition or situation, dissolving whatever needs dissolving, resolving whatever needs resolving.

God knows. God is there. God loves you. God cares. God is present and active now. You can be sure of it. Let go and let God take over. God is taking care of it.

The promise is: *Behold, the Lord's hand is not shortened, that it cannot save, or his ear dull, that it cannot hear....* (Isa. 59:1) Yes, dear friend, you can count on it. God is taking care of it now.

God is taking care of it. This has been a miracle-working prayer for me personally in the past year. On one occasion, upon awaking in the night, I felt anxious about the demands and pressures of the preceding days and weeks. I wondered how I was going to be able to cope with the challenges facing me. Suddenly the words *God is taking care of it* came to mind and I began thinking of the words of Jesus as He spoke to His disciples, reminding them: *"... the Father who dwells in me does his works."*

At that moment, I realized that I need not understand everything, that I need not meet every need of everyone, that I need not give all the answers, provide for all those whom I love and care about, because there is One who can and will. The Father abiding in each one will take care of it all. God is taking care of it in each life, through each circumstance, in each challenge.

For months after that particular experience, wherever I was—in my car, at the office, with others, or alone—at any moment that I became aware of the beginning of tension, anxiety, or concern, I quickly turned to the idea that God is taking care of it. I could instantly feel peacefulness returning. And amazing good resulted not only for me but for those around me.

On one occasion, a friend, who had found it necessary to be hospitalized, was told that she would never recover, that the case was hopeless. As we spoke over the telephone and knew together that *God is taking care of it,* she said that she felt a complete release and a feeling of inner contentment.

Within a few days she was home, continuing to know this same Truth in every detail concerning herself and her life. When she returned for a physical examination, the x-rays showed no sign of the disease. The physician told her that she was the most remarkable patient he had ever seen, that no one had ever gone through this same kind of experience with such a healthy attitude and with such positive results. He could not explain it and wondered if she could. Her response was simply, "God has taken care of it."

In another situation, a friend wrote: *Let me share with you the good news. My son just had a complete checkup and his blood pressure is the best it has ever been, his EKG is excellent, his cholesterol level is down to normal. His doctor was amazed and delighted. He said to my son, "Your body has had a complete reversal in the last year."* The mother had placed her son in the care of the Great Physician, knowing that He would take care of the healing need. God did take care of it.

This realization that God is taking care of it has continued to solve dozens of dilemmas for me, has brought about healing, peace, and needed support and supply. It has produced unique and unexpected answers to physical and material needs and continues to do so.

Doubt not, fear not, dear friend, but calmly and surely decree for yourself right now: *God is taking care of it.* You will find that marvelous blessings are at hand. God can handle all things better than you can imagine. God will take care of everything.

"I have made, and I will bear; I will carry and will save." (Isa. 46:4)

This is the moment to cease all fussing and fretting, to release all anxieties and personal concerns about yourself or anyone or anything. In place of this kind of negative thinking, let the pure life stream of the idea that God is taking care of it go to work for you and through you. Let its essence of wholeness sweep away every fear, wash away every doubt. Let its gentle power begin to dominate your thoughts and feelings until you become a clear channel through which God's thoughts and God's love can work.

Decree it and sing it; declare it and know it. God is taking care of it.

Morning, noon, and night, God is taking care of it.

Wherever you are, God is there in the midst of you, in the midst of the people around you, in the midst of the circumstance, in the midst of everyone and everything.

God is taking care of it all. God is taking care of it now. God is taking care of you.

If past mistakes appear to stand in the way of your good, remember that God is taking care of these situations, too. God is showing you the way to release and to let go the past, to live in the present, freely and happily. God is taking care of it.

If you are afraid of what might happen next week or next month or next year, remember again that *God is taking care of it.*

God loves you and has only good prepared for you. Be assured that God knows the desires of your heart and will fulfill them at the perfect time, in the perfect way. God's ways are ways of pleasantness and peace.

As you read these words accept the freeing thought that God is taking care of everything in your life. Let your physical being relax. Close your eyes to outer sights and appearances. Turn your attention to the loving Father within. Herein is the infinite supply of everything you can ever need or desire. Herein is your peace, assurance, renewed strength, patience, and understanding of yourself and others. Herein is the wellspring of love and joy, contentment and trust, faith and stability.

Softly and quietly repeat the words: *God is taking care of it,* and do not hesitate to say them again and again. Let anything you are especially concerned about come to light. As it does so, remind yourself that *God is taking care of it.*

If tension is felt in any part of your body, if thoughts of the past want to enter in, greet them with patience, again speaking aloud or silently: *God is taking care of it.* Continue to gently respond in this way to everything that seeks your attention.

Within a short time you will begin to feel relaxed and at peace. The past will no longer be a burden. The future will invoke no feelings of weight or worry. You will be free to live in the present moment, unhampered and unbound. You will find yourself thinking more clearly, sleeping more restfully, responding and reacting to others more calmly and patiently. You will be happier and more effective in all that you say and do.

God is taking care of it. As you continue to carry this little message with you into each experience, you will find a new world of cooperation all about you. You will no longer need to fight or struggle. You will be poised and centered in a spiritual stronghold within your own being. You will see things from a new perspective and from a point of view that is no longer critical or faultfinding. You will be at peace. You will feel the strength and power of God's presence at work within you and within your life.

Knowing that God is taking care of all things, you will find that you are more confident and capable than you had realized. Knowing that you are backed by God's love, supported by God's strength, guided by God's wisdom, you will rejoice in life and find good in every day. Knowing that God is taking care of each need will open the door of your heart to new miracles of healing.

Yes, dear friend, God is taking care of it.

God Will Turn It to Good

If you are concerned about some situation in your life, dear friend, know that God will turn it to good. If you feel that circumstances are against you, remember again, God will turn it to good.

God will turn the difficulty into advantage. God will sweep through the turbulent thoughts and emotions and conditions with a powerful wave of light and healing. God will turn everything to good.

The distressing appearances will change; God will turn all things to good. If you have not believed this, believe it now. If you have tried to believe this, then believe it even more. God will turn everything to good.

Decree this with firmness of faith. Decree it and boldly deny the reality or power of any appearance of lack or limitation.

God will turn it to good. God's power is infinite and it is present in your life right now. God's love is unceasing and it is at work in your personal affairs now. God's peace and strength are where you are every moment of the day or night. Neither event nor circumstance to the contrary, nor depth of despair, can prevent God's transforming presence and power from turning disadvantage to advantage, wrong to right, confusion to order, dilemma to divine guidance.

God will turn it to good. Believe this with all your heart. Believe this with all your mind. Believe this with all your being. God, your Father, loves you and is at work in and through all things to produce solutions that will bless everyone involved.

God will turn it to good. You need not know how or when or by what means. Trustingly, as a child, believe it. Choose to believe, choose to continue to believe, and choose to find peace and healing through believing.

If you have thought of negative conditions as being powerful, deliberately reverse your thinking, and align it with the mountain-moving power of God. *God will turn it to good.* The more often you speak these words, the stronger you will become, the more secure you will be in the faith that good is on the way in overflowing measure and from every direction.

You are not alone in meeting the changes and challenges of life. Your heavenly Father is with you and He is already clearing your way, opening closed doors, and removing every impediment and obstacle from your path.

God will turn it to good. Rely on God's presence rather than upon any individual or any particular happening you may have felt was needed for the fulfillment of your desires. Throw the weight of your faith upon God's power, and cease giving strength to opposing or conflicting elements. Trust God to do the work, to open the windows of heaven within your own mind to the right ideas and wisdom, to think through you, to function through you, and to turn everything to good.

A young man I know had to release a person who meant to him, at that time, total happiness and fulfillment. He was discouraged and disillusioned, but determined to hold on to the idea that God would turn it to good. He purposely filled the days and months that followed with prayer, knowing that God would turn it to good. He did not know by what means or how or when things would change in his life, but they did. New avenues of love, joy, and creativity opened in every area of his life. Life became interesting, exciting, and rewarding. Today he radiates total well-being and happiness. He smilingly says to anyone who asks for encouragement, "Believe it. God will turn it to good."

God will turn it to good. This was in essence the undergirding power that parted the seas for Moses. It was the nature of the armor that clothed David safely as he overcame Goliath. It was the basis for the food and water supplied Elijah and others as they struggled to cope with drought. It was the supporting substance that filled the baskets with loaves and fishes for the multitude. It was the underlying substance beneath Jesus' feet when He walked on the water. It was the element and substance of healing that blessed those in need of life and wholeness. As God turned all of these challenges to good, so He continues to do now for you and me and anyone who looks to Him as the one Source, the one Presence, the one Power. God is ready to turn everything in your life to good. As God's beloved offspring, nothing is impossible to you. No matter what it is in your life that seems lacking in possibilities for improvement, it can be turned to good.

A friend found this to be true in her life experience. Some years ago she was faced with rearing a child alone, with the necessity for finding some means of livelihood. The situation was an unhappy one that seemed to foster insecurity and lack of confidence and seemed impossible of producing anything good. Her inner fortification, however, came through, knowing that God would turn it to good. This belief provided daily support and gave her a higher vision of herself. Within a short while new channels of service opened to her and a rich and satisfying way of life unfolded. Step-by-step, everything that appeared negative and minus became positive and plus. God turned it all to good. Her face shows it, her attitude proves it, and her life reflects it to the upliftment and blessing of all who know her.

God will turn it to good. God gives ... *beauty for ashes, the oil of joy for mourning, the garment of praise for the spirit of heaviness . . . .* (Isa. 61:3 A.V.) God reassures you, saying: *Fear not... No weapon that is formed against thee shall prosper* and *... my kindness shall not depart from thee, neither shall the covenant of my peace be removed....* (Isa. 54:4, 10, 17 A.V.)

In my own experience, I have found invaluable this realization that God will turn it to good. It has brought harmony out of trouble and dissension, peace out of uncertainty and doubt, healing out of sickness, strength and conviction out of feelings of panic and fear.

In one critical challenge when it seemed as though everything was heading in the wrong direction, I held firmly to the belief that God was turning it to good. Love and understanding were revealed, confusion turned to harmony and cooperation. It was as though a wave of love swept through everyone and everything, personal striving ceased, and all was turned to good. God had turned it to good.

Yes, dear friend, God will turn it to good for you. God is your inner guidance and direction, your innate life and harmony and wellbeing; God is the all-providing Presence at hand to meet your every need.

God will turn it to good. You may find that some of your answers come quickly and clearly, others more gradually. Regardless, do your part, decreeing the Truth that God will turn it to good. Secure yourself in this reality, then do whatever is at hand to be done. Go the extra mile and give the extra love, share the added peace you need to share with others. Persistently detach yourself from old habits of hesitancy and doubt. Day by day go all the way in a total conviction that God will turn it to good.

God in You Is Coming Through

God in you is coming through! Wherever you find yourself in life, dear friend, God in you is coming through, right there, in that place, in that event, in that circumstance.

God in you is coming through without delay. You need not fear, for God is coming through where you are, bringing peace, courage, reassurance, light, guidance, and all else you desire.

God in you is coming through! Let this idea become a strong conviction within your mind and heart, and you will find greater blessings than you have ever before experienced.

One friend, in need of specific guidance in making a change, held to the thought: *God in*

me is coming through, and direct revelation
resulted, leading to orderly adjustment and
happy fulfillment.

For another person, desperately seeking to
sell highly-priced property quickly, the realization *God in me is coming through* brought
a satisfactory sale, completed within a week,
at a time when sales were known to be slow.

A woman, alone and discouraged in a
hospital, turned to prayer, knowing that
somehow in that very place God in her was
coming through. She continued to know this
in spite of appearances. She said later that at
one point suddenly a radiant light began to
envelop her in a peaceful warmth. This feeling
remained with her for days afterward. The
healing was a reality, and she was released
from the hospital with a continuing awareness of wholeness and well-being.

God in you is coming through! Instead of
being timid or hesitant, insist upon your
good, realizing that this is your divine birth-
right. You are the one who is to make the call,
to ask and seek and knock as often as you
need in order that the old shells of limitation
and unbelief may be broken and God may
come into expression through you. Your part,
so important right now, is your persistent

determination to claim and accept your good.

A friend wrote recently in honest admission: *I have been using the decree: "God in me is coming through," as you suggested and have in the process discovered things about myself that I have needed to understand. I found that in the midst of affirming this, all kinds of doubts and fears and feelings of inadequacy began to surface. Tears spilled out over the childishness of these feelings. After this, however, I could more freely continue with greater effectiveness in my prayers. I found myself telling the Father how much I wanted to believe, to be my best self, to be courageous, loving, strong, compassionate with myself as well as with others. I then began to feel something responding within me, giving assent to my every positive thought and word. It was as though the Father was patting me on the back for making the effort, for not giving up.*

Knowing this person well, I could see a miraculous happening taking place in his spiritual unfoldment. It brought not only a physical healing but opened up a new communication between him and the indwelling Father. Nothing has been the same in his life since that experience. God is coming through him as greater strength and accomplishment than ever before. So it can be for anyone who will recognize the power that lies within, who knows the Truth that God is coming through.

When Jesus said: *"I am the way, and the truth, and the life,"* He was giving us a proclamation of spiritual freedom to hold to and consider within the depths of our minds and hearts. Jesus' authority and command over life demonstrate the way each of us is to recognize and accept and follow the spiritual path. The Christ Way is demanding but wonderfully rewarding. It asks all the dedication and concentration of our faith, but it promises unlimited good in return.

God in me is coming through. I have found that this acknowledgment in the face of any test immediately diminishes the doubts and fears and brings forward an attitude of authority needed for overcoming. Using the affirmation: *God in me is coming through,* helps me to realize that I do not pray or work alone, that there is a power coming through me which will surmount any obstacle and bring the victory.

God in me is coming through. This declaration has hastened healing, guided me in handling details of home and work, kept me peaceful during stressful incidents, and revealed new understanding about myself and my relationship to my Father. It can do the same for you. God in you will come through in every need. Tell yourself right now:

God in me is coming through as perfect health and well-being.

God in me is coming through as my divinely appointed job.

God in me is coming through as my inner peace and security.

God in me is coming through as right companionship and love.

God in me is coming through as abundant supply and prosperity.

Take firm hold on this affirmation: *God in me is coming through.* Use it specifically for your own personal needs. Speak the words with the greatest conviction you can muster. That conviction will increase. Support it with the degree of faith that you now have. That faith will strengthen and grow. Be as firm with yourself as you can be in refusing to listen to any of the complaints or negative thoughts and feelings that call for your attention. Remember, you are following Jesus' advice to ask and seek and knock.

Having done all, move on about your appointed tasks, expecting and thanking the Father for the good that is on its way. Miracles will happen, changes will take place, blessing upon blessing will result. God in you is coming through!

Trust the Spirit Within

Trust the Spirit within, dear friend, to help you relax and let go. Trust the Spirit within to increase your health, happiness, and contentment.

Trust the Spirit within to bring you refreshing rest, sleep, and renewal each night. Trust the Spirit within to reveal to you right companions and satisfying relationships. Trust the Spirit within to pave the way to effective action and enjoyable living.

Trust, truly trust, the Spirit within.

Your trust frees you from burdens and releases you from feelings of excessive responsibility. To trust the Spirit within enhances the working of your intellectual processes and helps you perceive when the suggestions of others are wise and right for you. To trust the Spirit within brings you inner freedom from heaviness of thought and emotion and lifts you above the strain of difficult striving.

Practice momently trusting the Spirit within to reveal to you what you need to know. Trust the Spirit within to direct you in helping your body adjust to healing, strengthening, rebuilding. Trust the Spirit within to guide you into the most helpful ways of communicating with your family, into relating successfully to any challenge in home or business. Trust the Spirit within to unfold your life plan, and trust the Spirit within those whom you love to unfold their life plan to them.

In this process of trusting you will find, as I have, that anxiety is dissolved and that decisions come through more easily for you. You will find yourself less troubled about the future and more peaceful about the present. Your trust in the Spirit within will improve your attitudes, lighten worry, and bring you into a closer awareness of the presence of God within you.

Several years ago I found myself becoming anxious about a move that was imminent within the family circle. It involved physical work, adjustment, decisions, and demanded time and energy. Because so many doubts and apprehensions arose in this regard, the affirmation: *I trust the Spirit within,* was like an anchor, keeping my faith steady and secure. Again and again, these words were repeated to keep attention upon the Truth that the Spirit was within—within me, within the persons involved, within the situation.

In an unexpectedly short while everything was accomplished smoothly and easily, without undue burden or strain. My trust in the Spirit within produced quick action, clear guidance, and a harmonious and happy conclusion for all involved in every part of the move.

Trust the Spirit within to give you the right ideas to solve anything in your life that needs solving. Trust the Spirit within to illumine your mind. Trust the Spirit within to heal your body. Trust the Spirit within to release you from limiting relationships or habits. Trust the Spirit within to free you from agitation or irritation in regard to the attitudes of others. Trust the Spirit within to quiet your impatience and bring new peacefulness to your soul. Trust the Spirit within to show you how to handle your business, to give you guidance in making decisions, to fill you with a feeling of well-being.

Many people have been blessed and healed and helped through the use of this simple affirmation: *I trust the Spirit within.* In one instance a young friend was able to release a persistently difficult relationship, finding new inner peace and outer harmony in his life. His consistent decree: *I trust the Spirit within*, brought improvement in every way, including increased prosperity and interesting new activities.

Another person, faced with possible surgery, followed this same pattern of thought, trusting the Spirit within. She moved through each step of the challenge peacefully and the doctors released her within a short time. There was no need for surgery since the preoperative examination showed only that all was well—the difficulty had dissolved.

Again, a friend whose pet had been on medication without any sign of relief began to use the statement: *I trust the Spirit within to take care of you.* He said that he repeated the words often and took five minutes at a time to concentrate upon the affirmation rather than the appearance. Within a few

137

hours the condition improved, and within a few weeks it had totally disappeared.

In still another instance, a husband who had been anxious about his wife's apparent lack of wisdom in caring for herself, told me that this affirmation had worked in a miraculous way for him. He said that each time he became upset, he decreed repeatedly, silently: *I trust the Spirit within you to show you the way to help yourself.* He said, "It helped me to become calmer, and then she responded. She has taken proper care, used good judgment, without my saying one word outwardly. Everything is better as a result."

Trust the Spirit within—within yourself, within others, within any situation or circumstance confronting you. Trust the Spirit within your business ventures, within everything around you, within the weather, the plane in which you fly, the car in which you drive, or the environment in which you live. If you think that your faith is not adequate or your belief not strong enough, start to build that faith and belief with these very words, saying them boldly and firmly: *I trust the Spirit within.*

Practice trusting God, practice trusting His presence in you, practice trusting God's presence in others. Practice and continue practicing. Repeat the words: *I trust the Spirit within,* then let go. Discipline yourself to affirm this at the very moment you become upset or disturbed about something. Use the wonderful tools of your mind and heart positively and constructively and stay with the affirmative attitude of trusting the Spirit within until you begin to feel an inner response. It will come.

This affirmation: *I trust the Spirit within* has helped me to be calm instead of upset, quiet instead of angry, peaceful instead of irritated. It has brought me healing, guidance, increased blessings within and without, and is still doing so. It has relieved anxiety about those dear to me, helped me to release undue concern regarding any and every situation that could be difficult. It has opened up new ways and means to be helpful to myself and to others. It has kept me on the wavelength of positiveness and strength and courage, and it will do the same for you. Decree it now for yourself: *I trust the Spirit within.*

No matter how deep your difficulty appears to you, trust the Spirit within to guide you to victory. It will. If at first you find it a strug-

gle to trust, trust anyway. If you feel that it
is impossible for you to trust, trust anyway.
If you think you cannot make the grade, trust
the more. If you doubt your own ability,
potential, or capacity of faith, just be the
firmer and more insistent that you can trust
the Spirit within. Trust again and again and
again. Trust by the moment. Trust in the
morning, trust every hour on the hour, trust
at work and at rest. Trust yourself, trust
others, trust life, trust the Spirit in everyone
and in everything. The reality of the Spirit of
God lies within all, worthy of trust.

It was this kind of trust that led Simon
Peter to follow the Master's advice to launch
into the deep and let down the nets for the
desired catch of fish. Even though Peter had
already done that very thing earlier without
results, he followed anyway, trusted anyway,
believed in the Spirit as being greater than
the unproductive situation. As a result of this
total trust he was, we are told, astonished at
the catch of fish.

You, dear friend, stand upon the brink of
your good at this moment. It is there, right
where you are now. Begin to accept and receive it, first mentally and within your heart
by fully trusting the Spirit within. Declare

often, to deepen this acceptance: *I trust the Spirit within.* You will be following the direction of the One who knew the way to receive the very best of the kingdom of good. You will be launching into the deep with greater awareness of the good that lies ready and waiting for your acceptance in faith.

Trust the Spirit within!

Let the Divine Plan Unfold

Do you long for a perfect outworking of some challenging personal relationship? Be assured that there is a divine plan of love and understanding for you. Let go and let it unfold.

Do you need to know the right steps to take in making a decision? Be assured that there is a divine plan of light and guidance for you. Let go and let it unfold.

Do you pray to overcome a mental, emotional, or physical problem? Be assured that there is a divine plan of help and healing for you. Let go and let it unfold.

Do you want to attain greater understanding of yourself, to be happier, to be free from tensions and anxieties? Be assured that there is a divine plan of release, peace, and freedom for you. Let go and let it unfold.

Become inwardly quiet and turn your attention away from the demands of your everyday activities. Affirm: *There is a divine plan at work in my life. I now relax, let go, and let it unfold.* Listen attentively, inwardly, without projecting any thoughts about what you think should happen or be experienced. Become as a child, trusting and receptive to the Father abiding within, remembering that He is doing the work.

Perhaps answers will come instantly in these moments of quiet listening. An inner reassurance may be felt. Perhaps you will be moved to take some definite form of action. You may be guided to make a phone call, to talk to a particular person, or to write a letter. Or perhaps you may feel that you are to wait patiently upon the Lord for guidance. Do not question why specific answers have not come through. Instead, continue to know that there is a divine plan at work in your life.

Knowing that there is a divine plan at work in my life, I have often found answers and direction coming quickly. With this prayer as the basis, I was guided on a trip that I had been hesitant to take. Every detail was in divine order and every day revealed the unfolding of the divine plan.

In another instance, when no light seemed to be forthcoming, I affirmed: *There is a divine plan at work in my life. I let go and let it unfold.* Shortly thereafter I was guided to play a cassette tape that I had made for myself several weeks previously. I could hardly believe what I was hearing! Every thought expressed on the tape was a clear and direct answer to the questions I thought had not been answered. It was evident that the divine plan had been active without my being aware of it. All that was needed was my own quiet listening and inner seeing.

At another time, after seeking and knocking and asking prayerfully for guidance, I decreed firmly and with authority and in full faith: *There is a divine plan at work in my life. I now let go and let it unfold.* The following day a number of events converged into a divinely ordered happening that unmistakably pointed the way for me to go. Some aspects were not totally to my liking. Yet very quickly, many good things emerged from the experience that could not have come in any other way. It was beyond doubt the unfolding of a divine plan of good, boundless good, for me.

Assume right now, regardless of how you feel about it, that there is a divine plan of good at work in your life. As you assume this attitude of mind and heart, you will feel God moving through you in wonderful, at times mysterious, ways to bring about the best solution to your problems, the most helpful answers to your questions, and the most beneficial results for all concerned.

If your need is one of finances, remember that there is a divine plan at work in your affairs. Then let go and let it unfold. If you are meeting a physical or emotional challenge, know that there is a divine plan of healing at work in your mind and body. Let go and let it unfold. If your need concerns setting aright some important relationship, take heart and know that there is a divine plan at work in this circumstance. God will direct your every step. He will tell you when to be silent, when to speak. He will reveal His presence and show you how to handle any situation in love and wisdom to bring about right results. The divine plan of right relationships will become a reality to you as you let go and let it unfold.

There surely were times when even the

Master needed to remind Himself that a divine plan was a work in His life, times when He prayed earnestly and trusted the Father to bring about the clear direction desired. Jesus proved the power of such trust, the miracle-working power of letting the divine plan unfold through Him for all humanity.

Relax and let go your doubts, fears, anxieties, and tensions about anything in your life. Let go and let the divine plan of good unfold. Surrender your thoughts, your feelings, your entire being to the divine plan. Remember that there is a divine plan for the right outworking of every smallest detail, every greatest need and desire. Stand fast in the awareness that there is a divine plan at work in your life.

There is nothing you cannot approach in courage and wisdom, nothing you cannot cope with intelligently, nothing you cannot see your way through and rise above victoriously as you hold steadily to the Truth that God's divine plan is working throughout every experience of your life. Moment by moment that good plan is at work. Day by day it is unfolding. You will feel the Father's presence and you will see good revealed with each step you take.

You Can Be Free!

You can be free, dear friend. You can be free from worry and anxiety, from doubts and fears. You can be free from unhappy situations, from lack and limitation, from anything negative or undesirable.

You can be free from any binding circumstance, past or present, from any restricting condition, from turmoil, confusion, or destructive feelings. Be assured that freedom can come quickly without a long period of waiting until all outer things are set right. You can be free now.

This freedom begins within your thought—one thought at a time. Freedom is your spiritual birthright. There is nothing that can keep you tense, bound, or imprisoned when you know the Truth of your being.

At one time in my personal life when I needed to feel free from worldly pressures, I watched pelicans diving for their noonday catch of fish near the ocean's shore. Within a short while a dozen of the birds began to soar inland on a current of air high above, circling around the turrets of a large beach hotel. Once swept into the accessible current of air, they ceased all flapping of their wings and simply rested, sailing gracefully, circling endlessly, effortlessly, peacefully.

Although on the ground the pelicans appear awkward, once they have exercised the strong sweep of their wings they are beautiful to behold, an example of grace combined with skill in their intelligent cooperation with the elements. This scene aroused anew my awareness that as a child of God I have wings of faith to use to lift me into the desired freedom.

On that particular day as I watched the pelicans, I imagined myself in the process of stretching my wings of faith. I felt myself "flapping" my wings. I visualized myself rising above all the pressures of the world to a waiting current of God's love, ever ready to uphold and support me as I lifted my thoughts. I saw myself then resting upon the love of God, letting it carry me, lead me, direct me as I trusted it, rested within it and upon it. I could feel myself sailing, circling, upheld in an effortless movement of good. The heaviness and strain were gone. Peace and assurance prevailed.

Since then this same process of visualization has helped me time and again in knowing that I can be free. It has helped me open my mind to the Truth that I am a spiritual child of a spiritual Father, living in a spiritual universe, governed by spiritual law. It has helped me to remember that I am being led into new understanding and freedom in the midst of worldly appearances to the contrary. It has reminded me to open myself to the light of God's love. It has encouraged me to accept the concept of total freedom now.

This healing meditation and visualization has been a profoundly cleansing, renewing experience as I have practiced it. In each period of quietness, a new release comes through and a new freedom is felt. Challenging experiences have actually led me into new freedom and new awakening to the Truth that I can be free in spite of what happens outwardly.

Benefits have manifested in a number of important areas in my life and a new world of freedom has opened up gradually but increasingly.

You do not have to wait for next week or month or year or until all your challenges are dissolved or removed from your life. You can be free now. This freedom begins within your mind, within the innermost self of you.

To help bring this about, begin now to practice the three simple steps outlined for you here:

1. Quietly visualize the flight of the pelican.

2. Realize that you have wings to use. "Flap" these wings by decreeing: *I am free with the freedom of Christ.*

3. Finalize your acceptance of freedom as you rest upon the spiritual current of Truth and trust it to set you free.

As you practice these steps, you will become more peaceful, you will feel more secure, even before any outer change takes place. You will feel an increased awareness that no one and no thing can bind you or restrict your good. Former resentment toward some person or toward some situation will dissolve. You will realize that true inner freedom is not only a possibility and your spiritual birth-right but is the basis of the well-being for which you have longed.

You will no longer be traveling in the circle of telling yourself: "When my family is set-tled and happy, I'll be free." "When I have more time to enjoy life, I'll be free." "When I am out of debt, I'll be free." You will find yourself thinking in a new way about yourself and others and about your life. You will see that freedom is here for you now, not some day in the future, that it is not contingent upon some change in circumstances.

You will be inwardly satisfied, more con-tent, because you will no longer be caught up in the demands of the world. You will have a greater understanding of what the true pur-pose of your life is, your goals will be clearer, and your progress more rapid, more reward-ing.

One of the most remarkable aspects of the Master of freedom, Jesus of Nazareth, was His unbounded freedom with respect to per-sonalities, places, circumstances, and events. He pointed constantly to the fact that it is Truth and our inner knowing of it that sets us free. He puts it directly and unmistakably in the words: "*. . . you will know the truth, and* *the truth will make you free."* (John 8:32)

H. Emilie Cady in *Lessons in Truth* states: *Everyone wants to be free, free, free as the birds of the air—free from sickness, free from suffering, free from bondage, free from poverty, free from all forms of evil; and he has a right to be; it is a God-given desire, and a God-given right.*

As you comprehend this heritage, visualize it, realize it, and finalize it within your heart. Meditating upon it daily, you will find your freedom. You will know surely, strongly, powerfully, joyously, "I can be free! I can be free now! I am free!" And so shall it be!

About the Author

Since 1944 Mary L. Kupferle's articles have appeared in *Unity Magazine*, *Daily Word*, and other Unity publications. An ordained Unity minister, Reverend Kupferle has influenced thousands through her writings. She made her transition in April 2003.

Her other books of inspiring articles include the popular *Trust in the Goodness of God* and *Your Help Is at Hand*. Through all her writings, Mary Kupferle shared her finely tuned awareness of the presence of God in all situations.

Printed in the U.S.A.

B0180